WATER IN THE WILDERNESS

HARVARD SEMITIC MUSEUM

HARVARD SEMITIC MONOGRAPHS

edited by
Frank Moore Cross

Number 40
WATER IN THE WILDERNESS
by
William Henry Propp

William Henry Propp

WATER IN THE WILDERNESS
A Biblical Motif and Its Mythological Background

Scholars Press
Atlanta, Georgia

WATER IN THE WILDERNESS
A Biblical Motif and Its Mythological Background

William Henry Propp

Library of Congress Cataloging in Publication Data

Propp, William Henry.
Water in the wilderness.

(Harvard Semitic monographs ; 40)
Bibliography: p.
1. Water in the Bible. 2. Bible. O.T.—
Criticism, interpretation, etc. I. Title. II. Series.
BS1199.W22P76 1987 221.6'4 87–16314
ISBN 1-555-40157-0 (alk. paper)

Printed in the United States of America
on acid-free paper

For my family: Theodore, Ellen, James, Sharman, Donna and Stella Honig

TABLE OF CONTENTS

ACKNOWLEDGEMENTS

This work began its life as a seminar paper written in 1982; by 1985 it had developed into a doctoral dissertation directed by Frank M. Cross of Harvard University, and the published version is a revision of that thesis. I wish to express my deep gratitude to Professor Cross and to others from whose comments the manuscript has profited: principally, Michael D. Coogan, Paul D. Hanson, Richard E. Friedman, Baruch Halpern and Ronald S. Hendel. I wish also to thank R. A. Carlson, who, through our chance meeting in Sweden, awakened my interest in biblical studies, and my teachers William L. Moran and Thomas O. Lambdin, whose influence may not be adequately reflected in this book. Finally, I am grateful to the University of California, San Diego and to the Jerome and Miriam Katzin Publication Fund of the University's Judaic Studies endowment for funding the production of this volume.

William H. Propp
April, 1987

ABBREVIATIONS

AHW	W. von Soden, *Akkadisches Handwörterbuch*
AJSLL	*American Journal of Semitic Languages and Literature*
AnBib	Analecta Biblica
ANET	J. B. Pritchard, ed., *Ancient Near Eastern Texts Relating to the Old Testament*
AnOr	Analecta Orientalia
AOAT	Alter Orient und Altes Testament
ATD	Das Alte Testament Deutsch
BDB	F. Brown, S. R. Driver and C. A. Briggs, *Hebrew and English Lexicon of the Old Testament*
BHS	*Biblia Hebraica Stuttgartensia*
BKAT	Biblischer Kommentar: Altes Testament
BZAW	Beihefte zur *ZAW*
CAD	*The Assyrian Dictionary of the Oriental Institute of the University of Chicago*
CBQ	*Catholic Biblical Quarterly*
CTA	A. Herdner, ed., *Corpus des tablettes en cunéiformes alphabétiques découvertes à Ras Shamra-Ugarit de 1929 à 1939*
DJD	Discoveries in the Judean Desert
G	Old Greek Version
GKC	*Gesenius' Hebrew Grammar* (ed. E. Kautzsch, tr. A. E. Cowley)
HSM	Harvard Semitic Monographs
HUCA	*Hebrew Union College Annual*
IEJ	*Israel Exploration Journal*
JAOS	*Journal of the American Oriental Society*
JBL	*Journal of Biblical Literature*
JNES	*Journal of Near Eastern Studies*
JSOT	*Journal for the Study of the Old Testament*
JTS	*Journal of Theological Studies*
KAI	H. Donner and W. Röllig, *Kanaanäische und aramäische Inschriften*
KAT	E. Sellin, ed., Kommentar zum A.T.

KB	L. Kohler and W. Baumgartner, *Lexicon in Veteris Testamenti Libros*
LCL	Loeb Classical Library
OTL	Old Testament Library
OTS	*Oudtestamentische Studiën*
PEQ	*Palestine Exploration Quarterly*
PRU	*Le palais royal d'Ugarit*
RHA	*Revue hittite et asianique*
RHR	*Revue de l'histoire des religions*
SBS	Stuttgarter Bibelstudien
StudOr	Studia Orientalia
TLZ	*Theologische Literaturzeitung*
TWAT	G. J. Botterweck and H. Ringgren, eds. *Theologisches Wörterbuch zum Alten Testament*
UF	*Ugarit-Forschungen*
Ug	*Ugaritica*
VT	*Vetus Testamentum*
VTSup	*Vetus Testamentum*, Supplements
ZA	*Zeitschrift für die alttestamentliche Wissenschaft*
ZDPV	*Zeitschrift des deutschen Palästina-Vereins*
ZKT	*Zeitschrift für katholische Theologie*
ZTK	*Zeitschrift für Theologie und Kirche*

INTRODUCTION

Near Eastern mythic patterns exerted a profound influence on Israel's recitation of its national story.[1] In brief, it appears that the crossing of the Red Sea, the locus of the creation of the nation under the sovereignty of Yahweh,[2] was early associated with the mythic conquest of the primordial sea and the assumption of sovereignty over the dry land by Yahweh.[3] This creation tradition in turn derived from pre-Yahwistic myth, as we know from the thematically similar Epic of Ba'lu from Ugarit and Enūma Eliš of Babylon.

According to the Epic of Ba'lu,[4] after defeating Sea and, we presume, restricting him to the oceans, the storm god commissions Kôṯaru to construct a palace. This is more than a domicile and more than the celestial counterpart to an earthly temple: it seems to be the vault of the sky itself.[5] Though Ba'lu had initially intended the firmament to be impermeable, so that the earth would be deprived of life-giving showers, Kôṯaru convinces him to provide a window for precipitation. In other words, the conquest of Sea leaves the earth secure but sterile—the installation of the window completes the prerequisites for human existence.

The remainder of the myth also deals with the issue of fertility, telling of the repeated, but futile, battles of the storm god and Death. Both are killed and then resurrected. In other words, fertility and sterility are in constant competition, and neither can outpace the other.[6]

The Babylonian cosmogony Enūma Eliš[7] deals with similar matters. Having defeated the incursions of Sea (Tiāmat) and her cohorts, the storm god Marduk fashions the heavens and earth from Tiāmat's body, restricting the waters above with locks, yet allowing some to seep from her eyes and breasts to water the earth. Like Ba'lu, the newly enthroned Marduk commissions the building of a house, in this case the Esagila of Babylon. This text is less concerned with the conflict of fertility and sterility than the Ugaritic, partly because the inundation of the Euphrates and Tigris was more regular than the rains on which Syro-Palestinian agriculture depended, but also because Enūma Eliš is the more political of the two texts; its goal of aggrandizement of Babylon is not compatible with reflections on the limits of the power of the gods to bestow life.

In analyses of the reflexes of this mythic pattern in the biblical traditions of the Exodus, covenant and conquest, scholars have stressed the motifs of creation and sovereignty and slighted that of irrigation, i.e. fructification. Yet the Israelites could not have been less concerned with fertility than their polytheistic forebears, and one would *a priori* expect to find a promise of fertility in Israelite historical traditions.

This promise lies in the motif of the miraculous production of water in the desert. Though of seemingly minor significance in the prose sources, it occurs in poetry of all periods, from the archaic and highly mythological Psalm 114 to the archaizing and equally mythological Isaiah 34-35, 40-55. As is the case with the Red Sea traditions, mythological overtones are largely obscured in biblical historiography, appearing only when the prose texts are re-examined in the light of the poetic. This situation is to be expected. Biblical poetry is inherently more mythological than prose, since it frequently employs the Canaanite poetic formulary and, like myth, tends to simplify stories, eliminating details and even characters. One thinks of the scarcity of the mention of Moses in biblical poetry; Yahweh supersedes him as protagonist.

The mythological significance of the Water in the Wilderness motif may be simply expressed—it demonstrates the deity's power to sustain human, animal and vegetable life in the most inhospitable climes by the gift of water;[8] *a fortiori*, Yahweh may be expected to irrigate his own land. While a creation myth assures the world of fertility, the traditions under study here promise irrigation specifically to Israel.

Though the associations of the Water in the Wilderness motif with natural fertility are clear in many of the poetic references, the prose tradition historicizes the myth, telling how in a particular time and place Yahweh provided drinking water. This demythologizing occurs through a combination of two distinct types of story: 1)the myth of creation and fertility, and 2)the "historical" tale of divine succour in time of distress. Superficially, the prose accounts seem to belong wholly to type 2, while the poetic texts show a mixture. As we shall see, however, the Pentateuch (more precisely, the Elohistic source) associates its tales of miraculous springs with natural fertility in two ways, even if it does not describe the fertilizing of the desert: 1)it locates these springs at the mountain of Yahweh, 2)it links the motif of Water in the Wilderness to the theme of rebellion.

The connection of fertility and rebellion may not be obvious to the reader. In perusing the Bible, however, one is struck by the authors' constant suspicion of good fortune in general and fertility in particular. Many of the biblical writers share a conviction that a happy state is a temptation to sin; the Yahwist, in fact, opens his work with an exemplary tale of ingratitude in the midst of fertility (Genesis 2-3) and later tells of the iniquity and punishment of the inhabitants of Sodom and Gomorrah (Genesis 19), whose land was as fertile as the garden of Yahweh (Gen 13:10). Prophecies of prosperity in the land are often followed by predictions of or admonitions against sin, particularly the worship of other gods (e.g., Deut 6:10-15; 11:13-17; 31:20; Jeremiah 2; Ezekiel 16; Hos 13:1-8; Neh 9:25-26).[9] It is therefore no coincidence that the motif of the production of springs in the desert is linked to rebellion and, as will be shown, apostasy. And as rebellion in the wilderness is archetypical of rebellion in the land, and as the mountain in the desert represents the entire land of Canaan as well as its individual cult sites, and as the covenant in the desert is prototypical of the covenant of the tribes of Israel, so the provision of water in the desert contains a promise of water, i.e. fertility, in Canaan. Only such an interpretation can explain the motif's frequent appearance in poetry. As for the prose tradition, it downplays mythic motifs, as it does with the crossing of the sea, emphasizing Yahweh's gracious acts *in history* and avoiding direct reference to the fertilization of the desert. Nevertheless, it occasionally betrays mythic overtones.

I have endeavored in this study to devise a method that sensitizes us to the connections that exist between apparently separate traditions and accounts for the existence of divergent versions of the tale of the miraculous spring in the desert. My procedure differs from the Germanic and Scandinavian analysis of tradition-history developed in its fullest form by Martin Noth.[10] Noth believed that traditions (and frequently texts) form by a process of accretion, like crystals precipitating from a solution about a seed. Internal reconstruction leads to the kernel, i.e., the original form of the tradition. I am aware of no parallels to this type of development, however. Common sense, not to mention Near Eastern epigraphic data, argues against the supposition that in late second millennium Canaan all stories were told so briefly.[11] It also seems obvious that unless a story originated in a single eyewitness account of an historical event, it has no original form, but can be traced back almost indefinitely.[12] That is, the story's development is a continuum, along which we glimpse assorted loci.[13] This continuum extends through both space and time; i.e., attested loci may differ because they are told by different, but contemporary narrators, or because they pertain to different eras. Only in the latter case is the analysis of tradition-*history* feasible; in the former, though we may analyse the tradition, we cannot confidently trace its development. But even when texts of different periods tell a story variously, we may wonder whether this reflects historical development or the narrators' predilections. Generally, our data are too meager for firm conclusions.

While Noth erred in believing that the history of traditions can be traced by a process of reduction to components, he was correct in pointing out the existence of such components.[14] These elements are the *theoretical* building blocks of traditional literature;[15] they may be used in varying combinations, but rarely appear alone. If they do, moreover, there is no reason to consider the simplest form the earliest form.[16] Sometimes it may be possible to trace through time the varying composition of a tradition, but only if there are many specimens, as in the case of the Exodus from Egypt.

We will never know the extent to which the biblical sources are traditional literature. We must allow for accurate historical recording, on the one hand, and free composition, on the other. Nevertheless, the traditional component is considerable, and even a seemingly unique aspect of a text probably had parallels not incorporated into the Bible. Sometimes study of other ancient literature will partially remedy our ignorance.

A case in point is the motif of the provision of water in the wilderness and the traditions associating this act with the days of Moses. The Tetrateuch contains four accounts devoted to this theme—Exod 15:22-26; 17:1-7; Num 20:1-13 and 21:16-18. For the reader's convenience I quote here Exod 17:1-7, the most significant of the four.

> [1]All the community of the children of Israel journeyed from the desert of Sin on their travels at the command of Yahweh, and they camped at Rephidim, but there was no water for the people to drink. [2]The people strove with Moses, saying, "Give us water that we may drink," but Moses said to them, "Why do you strive with me, and why do you test Yahweh?" [3]But the people thirsted there for water, and the people complained against Moses, saying, "Why did you take me from Egypt to kill me and my children and my cattle with thirst?" [4]So Moses cried to Yahweh, saying, "What can I do with this people; in a little while they will stone me!" [5]Yahweh said to Moses, "Pass before the people and take with you some of the elders of Israel, and your rod, with which you struck the Nile, go and take in your hand. [6]I will be standing before you there, on the mountain in Horeb. Strike the mountain, and water will come out of it, so that the people may drink." So Moses did, in the sight of the elders of Israel. [7]He called the name of the place Massah (Testing) and Meribah (Strife), on account of the strife of the children of Israel and because they tested Yahweh, saying, "Is Yahweh in our midst or not?"

The rest of the Bible makes repeated reference to the creation of water in the desert, sometimes without specifying a locale[17] and sometimes referring to Massah or Meribah.[18] Prophecy and psalmody dealing with return from exile are especially fond of the motif of Water in the Wilderness.[19] The frequency of this motif and its associated traditions calls for a detailed study, for we have the controls necessary for their analysis—ample parallels and citations spread over a long time. These biblical passages do not attach the same significance to the motif of Water in the Wilderness nor tell the story of Massah and Meribah in the same way. Rather, they present us with loci on a continuum, and we must utilize a method capable of rigorously analysing a vague phenomenon.

While there is no original form of a tradition, we may define an *ideal* form, one that contains elements found in the various renditions. This method differs from Noth's, which sought the one kernel that generated the renditions. We can vary the specificity of the ideal form by changing the number of features in our definition. By proceeding from least to most specific, we are made aware a story's resonances in its ancient milieu. Chapter one is accordingly devoted to the motif of divine creation of water in the desert, with no other restrictions. We find three primary associations of the motif—watering the thirsty, cosmogony and the closely associated theme of provision of universal fertility. In the second chapter, I add two more restrictions—that the water be granted to the generation of the Exodus or that it issue from a mountain designated as *ṣûr, selaʿ* or *ḥallāmîš*. With one exception, these parameters apply to the same texts. With greater specificity comes a new association—the theme of apostasy. Moreover, fertility is now not universal fertility, but the fertility of Canaan. The third chapter examines texts that associate the gift of water with a particular place. After examining the Marah and Beer accounts, I study poetic passages referring to Massah and Meribah and note that they seem largely unrelated to Exod 17:1-7 and Num 20:1-13. When we come to these prose passages, we will recognize that they are not typical (i.e., close to the ideal) renditions of the story, but idiosyncratic ones, adapted to the special interests of the narrators. We will be able to isolate the traditional components that E and P used in forming their own versions of the events at Massah-Meribah and explain the manner in which they employed them. In the final chapter I examine references to divine production of water by the psalmists and prophets of restoration, where the connections with creation and fertility return to the fore. In each of these sections I do not resist the temptation to delve into sundry questions of text and exegesis, but the reader must always remember that the chief interest lies in the relation of fertility myths to the "historical" tradition of Water in the Wilderness.

NOTES TO INTRODUCTION

[1]The seminal study on Israelite myth is H. Gunkel, *Schöpfung und Chaos in Urzeit und Endzeit* (Göttingen: Vandenhoeck & Ruprecht, 1895). On the relation of myth and history, see F. M. Cross, *Canaanite Myth and Hebrew Epic* (Cambridge, Massachusetts: Harvard, 1973), especially chaps. 1-7, and the literature cited therein.

[2]More properly, one of the two loci, the other being the covenant at Sinai/Horeb.

[3]See Cross, *Canaanite Myth*, 112-144.

[4]I accept the sequence of *CTA* 1-6 as found in H. L. Ginsberg's translation in *ANET*^{3}, 129-141 and presume a unity in their received form, however disparate their antecedents.

[5]According to *CTA* 4.5.118-119, Ba'lu's house is of vast dimensions; its window (*'urbt*), described as a "rift in the clouds" (*CTA* 4.7.18,23) from which Ba'lu thunders (*CTA* 4.7.29-31; cf. 4.5.68-71), is comparable to the "windows of heaven" (*'ărubbōt haššāmayim*) mentioned in the Bible (Gen 7:11; 8:2; 2 Kgs 7:2; Isa 24:18; Mal 3:10); see J. C. de Moor, *The Seasonal Pattern in the Ugaritic Myth of Ba'lu* (AOAT 16; Neukirchen-Vluyn: Kevelaer, 1971) 162, n. 1. Isa 24:18 is particularly relevant, since it describes the opening of a window, thunder and earthquake as in *CTA* 4.7.25-32. Finally, the *lbnt* (*CTA* 4.5.73) and *ṯhrm 'iqn'im* (*CTA* 4.5.81,96-97), "bricks" and "clear lapis lazuli" used in building Ba'lu's mansion, recall Exod 24:10, where Israel's leaders behold under Yahweh's feet *k^{e}ma'ăśē(h) libnat hassappîr ûk(^{e})'eṣem haššāmayim lāṭōhar*, "as it were a pavement of lapis lazuli, clear like the sky itself."

[6]For our purposes, it is immaterial whether the Ba'lu-Môtu myth reflects the annual cycle of seasons or some other pattern. On the whole, however, I find the seasonal approach the most convincing. For a survey see de Moor, *Seasonal Pattern*, 9-28.

[7]*ANET*^{3} 60-72, 501-503.

[8]On the symbolism of water in the Bible see P. Reymond, *L'eau, sa vie, et sa signification dans l'Ancien Testament* (VTSup 6; Leiden: Brill, 1958).

[9]This seemingly reflexive transition from predictions of weal to harsh warnings is probably a response to the perceived threat of agrarian paganism.

[10]*Überlieferungsgeschichte des Pentateuch* (Stuttgart: Kohlhammer, 1948). For a general discussion of this school see D. A. Knight,

Rediscovering the Traditions of Israel (SBL Dissertation 9; Missoula, Montana: Scholars Press, 1975).

[11] Contrast the remarks of H. Gunkel, *Genesis*^{3} (Göttinger Handkommentar zum Alten Testament 1.1; Göttingen: Vandenhoeck & Ruprecht, 1910) xxxii-xxxiv.

[12] Even an eyewitness might use traditional phraseology to narrate a contemporary event; see M. Eliade, *The Myth of the Eternal Return* (Bollingen Series 46; New York: Random House, 1965) 39-46. In such a case one can speak of an "original form" only with qualifications, depending upon the proportion of traditional material employed.

[13] See the chapter aptly titled "Songs and the Song" in A. B. Lord, *The Singer of Tales* (Harvard Studies in Comparative Literature 24; Cambridge, Massachusetts: Harvard, 1960) 99-123.

[14] Cf. Cross, "The Epic Tradition of Early Israel: Epic Narrative and the Reconstruction of Early Israelite Institutions," *The Poet and the Historian* (ed. R. E. Friedman; Harvard Semitic Studies; Chico, California: Scholars Press, 1983) 24-25.

[15] This type of analysis is commonly associated with the study of oral tradition, yet it may also be applied to written texts, ancient or modern.

[16] As Noth (*Überlieferungsgeschichte*, 137) did, for instance, in positing that the murmuring theme originated in the account of Kibroth Hattaavah (Num 11:4-35). While it is barely conceivable that a single Israelite storyteller began to tell stories about Israel's insubmission to Yahweh in the desert period and that such stories then became fashionable, it is inconceivable that any trace of this would be visible in the Bible as we have it. In fact, the murmuring theme, if it does not rise from historical memories of the Exodus, probably reflects the turbulence of the premonarchical period, when the traditions behind J and E took form.

[17] Deut 8:15; 32:13; Ps 78:15-16,20; 105:41; 114:8; Neh 9:15.

[18] Exod 17:1-7; Num 20:1-13,24; 27:14; Deut 6:16; 9:22; 33:8; Ps 81:8; 95:8; 106:32.

[19] Isa 35:6-7; 41:17-19; 43:20; 48:21; 49:10; Jer 31:9; Ps 107:3.

Chapter One
THIRST AND CREATION

Thirst Assuaged

At the simplest level, tales of assuaged thirst assured the Israelites that Yahweh had both the power and the disposition to furnish drinking water and in general succor people in desperate situations. Such stories constitute a minor literary genre, and we find many parallels in world folklore.[1]

There are several biblical examples besides those pertaining to the wilderness generation.[2] God, having heard the cry of Ishmael, directs Hagar to a well in Gen 21:19. In Judg 15:18-19, Samson, after defeating the Philistines,

> *18*thirsted sorely there, and he cried to Yahweh and said, "You have given to your servant this great victory, but now I (will) die of thirst and fall into the hand of the uncircumcised." *19*So God cleft the Grinder[3] of Lehi, and water came from it, and he drank, and his spirit returned, and he revived. Therefore he called its name the Well of the Caller[4] which is in Lehi until this day.

The pattern of the story could be described as thirst, complaint, cleaving of rock, drinking, naming the well; this is very close to the pattern of Exod 17:1-7 and Num 20: 1-13.

2 Kgs 2:19-22 is not, strictly speaking, a thirst story, nor does it take place in the desert, yet it deals with miraculous provision of water. The newly inaugurated Elisha, having crossed the Jordan dry-shod, comes to a town of which

> the water was bad, and the land prone to miscarriage. *20*He[5] said, "Get me a new vessel and put salt in it," and they brought it to him. *21*He went out to the water source and cast into it salt and said, "Thus says Yahweh, 'I have healed this water; there will no longer be in it death or miscarriage'."[6] *22*The water has been healed until this day.

The healing of the spring, following the crossing of the Jordan, seemingly alludes to the traditions recorded in Exodus 14-15, in which the Red Sea is crossed and the waters of Marah healed.[7]

Another miracle of Elisha involves the provision of drinking water and is a true thirst story. 2 Kgs 3:4-27 tells of the battle of Jehoram of Israel and Jehoshaphat of Judah against Mesha of Moab. Their armies travel through the Edomite desert and are joined by the forces of the king of Edom. When they had journeyed a week, however, "there was no water for the camp or for the animals in their train. The king of Israel said, 'Woe! Indeed Yahweh has summoned these three kings to give them into the hand of Moab'" (vv 9-10). Elisha is called, and he delivers an oracle: "Thus says Yahweh: 'This wadi is to be made nothing but cisterns.'[8] For thus says Yahweh: 'You will not see wind and you will not see rain, but that wadi will be full of water, and you will drink, you, your herds and your camp[9],'" (v 16-17). A prediction of victory over Moab follows. Then, "in the morning, at the time of the offering, there was water coming from the land of Edom, and the land was full of water" (v 20). This seems to be a description of the onset of a flash flood, but when the Moabites see the water redly reflecting the dawn, they assume it to be the blood of the armies shed in a falling-out and rush precipitously upon the enemy camp, only to be routed. In this story the water serves two purposes. It is requested to slake the thirst of the armies and their cattle, but the narrator does not describe their drinking. Its principal function in the story is rather to lure the Moabites to their deaths.

These four stories amaze the reader with the miraculous provision of water, expressing the hopes of a society dependent upon the erratic ground waters of Canaan. Such concerns are also voiced in hymnody: "He leads me to still waters...My cup overflows" (Ps 23:2,5). Yahweh himself may be described as a source of water.[10]

Creation and Fertility in Canaan and Israel

In arid climes, water is not just vital for drink, but it is the most important requirement of plant and animal life. H.

Gressmann conveyed the resonances of the imagery of desert springs in his description of the actual oasis of Massah, which he presumed motivated the etiological account of Exod 17:1-7: "He who goes there today finds delicious drinking water and consequently also shade trees. Thus, through the power of Yahweh and the magic rod of Moses, the former desert is converted forever into a garden of God, for, wherever water and trees are, there, for the Oriental, is blessedness and Paradise."[11] Worshippers of all religions demand of their gods water, not just for drink but for general fertility; the peoples of Canaan from whom the Israelites emerged in the Iron Age were no exception.[12]

As we may judge from both onomastics and myth, the two most important gods of the Canaanites were 'Ilu and Had(a)du, the latter often referred to as Ba'lu, "the lord." 'Ilu was the elder who embodied the authority of the gods, while Ba'lu was a younger deity who played a more vigorous role in the myths. Both are relevant to our topic.

'Ilu's residence, at times described as a mountain,[13] is at other times described as being "at the source of the two rivers, in the midst of the channels of the two deeps."[14] In a Hittite version of a Canaanite myth,[15] Elkunirsa (<* *'El-qōnē(y)-'arṣ*)[16] is said to dwell at the source of the Mala (Euphrates) river. 'Ilu is associated with water in its aspect as one of the chief constituents of the universe.

As his name implies, Ba'lu Had(a)du is a storm god.[17] As such, he is responsible for the waters that fall as precipitation and for the ground sources that are augmented during the rainy season. In his absence there is "no dew, no shower, no *šr'* of the two deeps, no sweetness of Ba'lu's voice."[18] In his Mesopotamian guise of Adad, Had(a)du also controls both the waters above and below.[19] In Islamic sources, land moistened by ground water is described as "watered by Baal."[20] Ba'lu is therefore associated with water in its aspect as agent of fertility.

The Old Testament finds many ways of associating Yahweh with waters of fertility. For instance, allusions to Creation mention that Yahweh assured that the world was amply irrigated:[21] "Yahweh founded the earth by wisdom, established the heavens with understanding; by his knowledge the springs were cleft, and the clouds drip dew" (Prov 3:19-20); "You [Yahweh] cleft spring and wadi; you dried perennial rivers" (Ps 74:15).[22] The most familiar examples of this motif are found in the opening of the Yahwistic document: "On the day that Yahweh Elohim had[23] made earth and heaven, there being as yet no shrub of the field and no grain of the field having yet sprouted, though[24] an *'ēd*[25] was rising from the earth to water all the surface of the soil, then Yahweh Elohim molded the human from the dirt of the earth..." (Gen 2:4b-7a). And again, below:

> *10*A river arises in Eden to water the garden, and from there it separates into four branches. *11*The name of one is Jumper [*Pîšôn*]; it circumvents/winds through[26] all the land of Havilah, where there is gold *12*(The gold of that land is good; resin and carnelian [?] are there). *13*The name of the second river is Gusher [*Gîḥôn*];[27] it circumvents/winds through all the land of Kush. *14*The name of the third river is the Tigris; it goes east of [the city][28] Assur. The name of the fourth river is the Euphrates (Gen 2:10-14).

The number four is significant. It represents totality, and it also recalls the double rivers and double deeps of 'Ilu's abode.[29] Note, too, that, like 'Ilu's home, Eden is presumed to be on a mountain, since water flows down-hill.[30] Ezekiel also refers to the ground waters of Eden (31:4,5,7), and he explicitly locates Eden on a holy mountain (28:14,16)[31] in Lebanon (31:3,15,16).[32]

We also find biblical texts referring not to Yahweh's creation of the world, but to his continued sustenance of it through water. These passages are of less interest to us, however, as they more often describe precipitation than springs or rivers. The context may be hymnody[33] or oracle.[34] It may be benediction[35] or polemic against other gods falsely believed to control fertility.[36] It may be a description of the rewards of covenant fealty.[37] Yahweh's theophany often includes precipitation, in imagery largely deriving from the the poetic canons of the Had(a)du cult.[38] Yahweh also demonstrates his power in a negative fashion, punishing humanity by withholding water.[39] While reference to sustenance of the world through ground waters is rarer,[40] it becomes the major motif in oracles of restoration of fertility following return from exile.[41] Most significant is the frequent description of the mighty river said to issue from Zion,

Yahweh's holy mountain.

> For Yahweh is powerful for us there,[42]
> A place of rivers,[43] wide[44] channels
> In which oared boats will not travel,
> Which a mighty ship cannot pass (Isa 33:21).
>
> *8b*Gods[45] and humans
> Shelter in the shade of your wings.
> *9*They are refreshed from the fat/sap[46] of your house,
> And you give them drink from your fertilizing brook,
> *10*For with you is a flowing source (Ps 36:8b-10a).
>
> There is a river whose channels fertilize[47] the city of God,
> the shrine[48] of the tent[49] of Elyon (Ps 46:5).
>
> The channel of God is full of water (Ps 65:10).
>
> He returned me to the door of the Temple, and water was running eastward from under the threshold (Ezek 47:1).
>
> On that day flowing water will go out from Jerusalem (Zech 14:8).
>
> A spring will arise in the house of Yahweh and water the wadi of Shittim (Joel 4:18).

This image is derived from the Canaanite description of the abode of 'Ilu.[50]

Summary

Gen 21:19; Judg 15:18-19 and 1 Kgs 3:4-27 tell how Yahweh provides water to thirsty individuals; in 1 Kgs 2:19-22 his proxy Elisha performs a magical healing of a spring. The stories are diverse in form, though the Samson account closely parallels the passages to be examined in chapter three. On the other hand, both Creation texts such as Genesis 2; Ps 74:15; Prov 3:19-20 and the Zion tradition stress Yahweh's role as irrigator and fertilizer, showing contacts with the myths of other peoples. We therefore expect to find mythological allusions in tales of Yahweh's creation of water in the desert.

1 In particular, the hero (or god) smiting a rock or the ground to create a spring is a common motif (Stith Thompson A941.3, D1549.5, 1567.4-6,). J. G. Frazer (*Folklore in the Old Testament* 2 [3 vols.; London: Macmillan, 1918] 463-364) cites an Indonesian tale resembling the traditions of Massah and Meribah. In Pausanias 4.36.7 and 3.24.2 we read of similar exploits of Dionysos and Atalante. Compare, too, Poseidon's creation of the spring of Athens with his trident; see the note of Frazer, ed., *Apollodorus—The Library* 2 (2 vols.; LCL; London: Heinemann, 1921) 78-79, n. 1.

2 The thirst stories of Marah (Exod 15:22-26) and Beer (Num 21:16-18) will be discussed in detail in chapter three.

3 Cf. the *maktēš* of Jerusalem (Zeph 1:11). On the long tradition of interpreting *maktēš* as "molar," see M. J. Lagrange *Le livre des juges* (Études Bibliques; Paris: Libraire Lecoffre, 1903) 244, n. 19. G^{A} translates *trauma*, "wound," and G^{B} *lakkos*, "pond." In Zeph 1:11, G has *katakekommenē*, "stump (?)." Apparently, the Alexandrians had a vague sense that *ktš* refers to destruction, hence *trauma* and *katakekommenē*, while *lakkos* was a later guess from context.

4 It is often proposed that the true meaning of *'ên haqqōrē'* is "Well of the Partridge." The suggestion originates with J. D. Michaelis, according to C. F. Burney, *The Book of Judges* [first published separately in 1918] *and Notes on the Hebrew Text of the Books of Kings* [1903] (New York: KTAV, 1970) 375.

5 G "Elisha" is an explanatory plus.

6 *M^{e}šakkelet* may refer to miscarriage (so, e.g., J. A. Montgomery, *The Books of Kings* [ICC; Edinburgh: Clark, 1951] 355) but is more likely to allude to agricultural sterility as in Mal 3:11 (J. Gray, *I & II Kings* [OTL; Philadelphia, Pennsylvania: Westminster, 1963] 427-428). The roots *mwt* and *škl* are also linked in Lam 1:20, and in *CTA* 23.8 we read that in the hand of Death (*Mt*) is *ḥṭ ṯkl*, "the scepter of bereavement."

7 See below, p. 52-53.

8 It is unclear if this is a command or a prediction; see the commentaries.

9 Reading **maḥănêkem* for MT *miqnêkem*, following the Lucianic recension of G.

10 Jer 2:13; 15:18 (negatively); 17:13; Ps 42:2; 63:2.

11 H. Gressmann, *Mose und seine Zeit* (Göttingen: Vandenhoeck &

Rupricht, 1913) 147.

[12]Nor were the Mesopotamians and Egyptians, who revered gods, Enki/Ea and Ḥ‘py (the Nile), among whose chief responsibilities was irrigation.

[13]*CTA* 2.1.14,20 (*ǵr*); 1.2.3,23, 3.11,22 (*hršn*). See M. Pope, *El in the Ugaritic Texts* (VTSup 2; Leiden: Brill, 1955), 61-72 and R. J. Clifford, *The Cosmic Mountain in Canaan and the Old Testament* (HSM 4; Cambridge, Massachusetts: Harvard, 1972) 35-57.

[14]*Mbk nhrm qrb 'apq thmtm* (*CTA* 2.3.4; 3.5.14; 4.4.21; 5.6.2; 6.1.33; 7.6.47), with a variant containing *b‘dt*, "meeting," for *qrb* in *Ug5* 7.3. This alternate version suggests that *qrb* might be an infinitive of *qrb*, "to approach," rather than a noun "midst." Many theories have been proposed as to the identities of these bodies of water; Pope (*El*, 72-81) thinks of the Nahr Ibrahim which supposedly emerges in separate flows at both Afqa and Yammuneh. T. H. Gaster (*Thespis*[2] [Garden City, New York: Doubleday, 1961] 183) suggests the waters above and below, nor should we exclude from consideration the salt and fresh waters. We could also see here four bodies of water, as that number expressed universality in the ancient world (cf. Hebrew *'arba‘ kanpôt hā'āreṣ*, Akkadian *kibrāt arbai[m]/erbetti[m]*). For depictions of two or four symmetrical streams, see H. Frankfort, *Cylinder Seals* (London: Macmillan, 1939) 88, fig. 29; 116, fig. 32; 143, fig. 37; 213, fig. 65; 219, fig. 66; A. Parrot, "Les peintures du palais de Mari," *Syria* 18 (1937) 335-346, esp. 335-337; M.-T. Barrelet, "Une peinture de la cour 106 du palais de Mari," *Studia Mariana* (ed. A. Parrot; Leiden: Brill, 1950) 16-17; Buchanan, *Catalogue of Ancient Near Eastern Seals in the Ashmolean Museum* 2 (2 vols.; Oxford: Clarendon, 1962) 102, 562 (pl. 38). Many literary parallels are given in W. F. Albright, "The Mouth of the Rivers," *AJSLL* 35 (1919) 161-195.

[15]See H. Otten, "Ein kanaanäischer Mythus aus Boǧasköy," *Mitteilungen des Instituts für Orientforschung* 1 (1953) 125-150, A. Goetze, "El, Ashertu and the Storm-god," *ANET*[3] 519 and H. A. Hoffner, "The Elkunirsa Myth Reconsidered," *RHA* 23 (1965) 5-16.

[16]See Otten ("Kanaanäischer Mythus," 136-137) and P. D. Miller, "El, The Creator of Earth," *BASOR* 239 (1980) 43-46.

[17]Cf. Arabic *hadda*, "beat, make noise," (compare Ethiopic *negwadgwād*, "thunder"). From the same root are Hebrew *hêdād*, "shout," and *hēd*, "noise." On the god himself, see A. S. Kapelrud, *Baal in the Ras Shamra Texts* (Copenhagen: Gad, 1952); P. J. van Zijl, *Baal* (AOAT 10; Neukirchen-Vluyn: Neukirchener Verlag, 1972).

[18]*Bl ṭl bl rbb bl šrʿ thmtm bl ṭbn ql bʿl* (*CTA* 19.1.42-6). We are not sure of the meaning of *šrʿ*. An identical word occurs in a list of fluids (*Ug5* 9.1.21) among oil, ointment, balm and honey, and hence our text may be metaphorically describing the ground waters as a precious fluid; cf. "fat of the earth" in Gen 27:28,39 and *CTA* 3.2.39-41; 3.4.87-8, paralleling "dew of heaven." Other examples of the metaphorical description of water as milk, honey etc. are discussed below, pp. 27-28. Another possibility is T. L. Fenton's ("Ugaritica-Biblica," *UF* 1 [1969] 67-68, n. 15a.) connection with Arabic *šaraʿa*, "to move in a direction" (cf. Ethiopic *šarʿa*, "to arrange"), yielding a translation such as "motion"; Fenton notes that Arabic *šarīʿatun, mašraʿatun* and Old South Arabic s^2*rʿ*, *ms*^{2}*rʿn* denote sources of water, though these may be local developments from a basic meaning "goal of a journey." Another potential cognate is be Hebrew *hôrîaʿ*, "shout," which makes good parallelism with "Baʿlu's voice" and recalls biblical descriptions of the shouting or singing of nature (Isa 14:7-8; 44:23; 49:13; 55:12; Hab 3:10; Ps 96:11-12; 98:7-8). Finally, F. M. Cross *apud* G. E. Wright ("The Lawsuit of God: A Form-Critical Study of Deuteronomy 32," *Israel's Prophetic Heritage* [Fs. J. Muilenberg; ed. B. W. Anderson and W. Harrelson; New York: Harper, 1962] 27) and also W. L. Moran ("Some Remarks on the Song of Moses," *Bib* 43 [1962] 322) propose a connection with *ś*^{e}*ʿîrîm* in Deut 32:2.

[19]See Code of Hammurapi 50.64-71, *Adad bēl ḫegallim gugal šamê u erṣetim rēṣūʾa zunni ina šamê mīlam ina nagbim līteršu* (R. Borger, *Babylonish-akkadische Lesestücke* 2 [3 vols.; Rome: PBI, 1963] 44), "May Adad, lord of bounty, canal inspector of heaven and earth, my helper, deprive him [the defacer of the inscription] of rain from heaven and seasonal flood from the deep," and *Atra-Ḫasīs* 2.1.11-3, *zunnīšu Adad lišaqqil šapliš ayyillik mīlu ina nagbi* (W. G. Lambert and A. R. Millard, *Atra-Ḫasīs* [Oxford: Oxford, 1969] 72), "Let Adad withhold his rain, below let no seasonal flood come from the deep." For other examples see B. Landsberger, "Jahreszeiten im Sumerish-Akkadischen," *JNES* 8 (1949) 259, n. 54 and A. Falkenstein, W. von Soden, *Sumerische und akkadische Hymnen und Gebete* (Bibliothek der alten Welt; Zürich/Stuttgart: Artemis, 1953) 280. For a recently discovered reference to Hadad as irrigator see A. Abou-Assaf, P. Bordreuil and A. R. Millard, *La statue de Tell Fekheryeh* (Études Assyriologiques 7; Paris: Recherche sur les civilisations, 1982) 23.

[20]See W. Robertson Smith, *Lectures on the Religion of the Semites*^{2} (London: Black, 1914) 96-99; R. Blachère, M. Chouémi and C. Denizeau, *Dictionnaire Arabe-Français-Anglais* 1 (Paris: Maisonneuve et Larose, 1967-) 723-724. A similar Rabbinic Hebrew

term, *bêt Ba'al*, refers to land watered by rain alone; see M. Tsevat, "The Canaanite God Sälaḥ," *VT* 4 (1954) 45-46.

[21]This is a feature of other Near Eastern myths; cf. Enūma Eliš 5.47-58 (*ANET*^{3}, 501-502) and "Enki and Ninhursag" 45-49, 55-60 (*ANET*^{3}, 38).

[22]On this passage as an allusion to Creation, see J. A. Emerton, "'Spring and Torrent' in Psalm LXXIV 15," *Volume du congrès, Genève, 1965* (VTSup 15; Leiden: Brill, 1966) 122-133, especially 130-133. Emerton plausibly conjectures that the springs were at first opened to dry up the primeval waters.

[23]The Yahwist, unlike P, does not begin with the creation of the Cosmos, i.e., "earth and heaven," but rather he presupposes it; see J. Skinner, *Genesis*^{2} (ICC; Edinburgh: Clark, 1930) 51.

[24]We are still in a subordinate clause, and the action begins with v 7; otherwise, the verb would be **wayya'al*. This is not an act of creation. Although the *'ēd* was presumably made before our story begins, it is now rising spontaneously. Hence I do not find M. Dahood's ("Eblaite *i-du* and Hebrew *'ēd*, 'Rain Cloud'," *CBQ* 43 [1981] 536) parsing of *ya'ăle(h)* as a Hiphil attractive.

[25]The G translates *'ēd* as *pēgē* and Aquila as *epiblysmos*, "spring," while the targumim have *'ănānā'*, "cloud." No convincing Semitic etymology has been proposed, and so we must rely upon context. The Greek rendering is to be preferred on four counts. First, it is more expected to describe springs or rivers, rather than clouds, as rising from the earth. Second, if the *'ēd* were a cloud, it would presumably moisten the earth through rainfall (unless one thinks of dew, as in Prov 3:20), which contradicts 2:5. Third, *hišqâ* is never used of clouds. In Job 36:27 the meaning "cloud" allegedly fits better, but since v 28b is to be translated "showers fall upon the earth" (M. Dahood, "Zacharia 9,1, *'Ên 'Ādām*," *CBQ* 25 [1963] 123-124), the parallelism of *lᵉ'ēdô* and *'ălê 'ādām* suggests that the former be rendered "into the ground water." Fourth, Ezek 31:4,5,7 (cf. Gen 13:10) refers to the ground waters of Eden. Most modern commentators have offered as further evidence in favor of the G one of two Sumerian etymologies. A. Dillmann (*Die Genesis*^{3} [Kurzgefasstes exegetisches Handbuch zum Alten Testament; Leipzig: Hirzel, 1892] 52) was the first to propose derivation from Akkadian *edû* (< *A.DÉ.A*), and more recently E. A. Speiser ("*'Ed* in the Story of Creation," *BASOR* 140 [1955] 9-11) has championed this view. M. Saebø ("Die hebräischen Nomina 'ed und 'ēd," *ST* 24 [1970] 131-134) raises convincing objections, however, chiefly on the grounds that *edû* refers to a destructive rush of water. Alternatively, many follow the derivation first proposed by P. Dhorme ("L'arbre de vérité et

l'arbre de vie," *RB* 4 [1907] 274) and E. Sachsse ("Der jahwistische Schöpfungsbericht," *ZAW* 39 [1921] 281-282) and buttressed by Albright ("The Babylonian Matter in the Predeuteronomic Primeval History (JE) in Gen 1-11," *JBL* 58 [1939] 102-103), from Sumerian *ÍD*, "river." This is phonologically and semantically more suitable, though "river" is not a typical loan word.

[26]The sense of *sōbēb* is unclear here.

[27]If this is to be equated with the spring of Jerusalem of the same name (1 Kgs 1:33,38,45; 2 Chr 32:30; 33:14), we would have another example of the belief that separate bodies of water are connected underground. Cf. the Arabic traditions cited by Pope (*El*, 77-80) and the description of the Tigris in Pliny (*Natural History* 6.128). Many medieval Bible readers drew just this conclusion; see H. R. Patch, *The Other World According to Descriptions in Medieval Literature* (Smith College Studies in Modern Languages, N.S. 1; Cambridge, Massachusetts: Harvard, 1950) 136-137, 144, 147, 149, 151. If the Gihon is supposed to be one of the great rivers, the best candidate is the Nile, which is equated with the Gihon in the G of Jer 2:18 (cf. Josephus, *Antiquities* 1.1.3). On the other hand, E. Meyer (*Die Israeliten und ihre Nachbarstämme* [The Halle: Niemeyer, 1906] 210) thinks that omission of the Nile is evidence of Mesopotamian origin.

[28]See Speiser, *Genesis* (AB 1; Garden City, New York: Doubleday, 1964) 17.

[29]See note 14.

[30]Gunkel (*Genesis*, 36) and U. Cassuto (*A Commentary on the Book of Genesis* 1 [2 vols.; Hebrew original 1944; Jerusalem: Magnes, 1961] 76-77), anticipated by Moses bar-Cepha (*apud* Patch, *Other World*, 147). Eden is to be considered a divine abode, rather than just a human abode, because of the presence of Yahweh in the garden even in J (Gen 3:8) and because of references elsewhere to the garden of Yahweh (Gen 13:10; Isa 51:3) or Elohim (Ezek 31:8-9).

[31]Hence the medieval location of Eden on a mountain; see Patch, *Other World*, 120, 138, 142, 146, 149, 151, 153, 154, 165, 185.

[32]The location of the garden of Yahweh in the Lebanese mountains was not Ezekiel's invention, for Ps 80:11; 104:16, the worship of an El-type deity called "Lord of the Amanus" (see Cross, *Canaanite Myth*, 24-28) and perhaps even the Old Babylonian account of the Cedar Forest in Lebanon, a divine abode guarded by a storm monster (see T. Bauer, "Ein viertes altbabylonisches Fragment des Gilgameš-Epos," *JNES* 16 [1957] 254-262 and J. H. Tigay, *The Evolution of the Gilgamesh Epic* [Philadelphia, Pennsylvania: University of Pennsylvania, 1982] 76-78) may reflect the same

tradition.

[33]Ps 104:13; 147:8; Job 5:10; 26:8; 28:25-26; 37:4-11; 38:22-30.

[34]Isa 30:23; Ezek 34:26; Joel 2:23; Mal 3:10.

[35]Gen 27:28.

[36]Jer 14:22; 1 Kings 17-18.

[37]Lev 26:4; Deut 11:14; 28:12.

[38]See Cross, *Canaanite Myth*, 147-194.

[39]Lev 26:19; Deut 11:17; 28:23-24; 1 Kgs 8:35 (=2 Chr 6:26); 17:1; Isa 5:6; Jer 3:3; Ezek 22:24; Hag 1:10-11; Zech 14:17; 2 Chr 7:13.

[40]Besides the creation accounts, we have Isa 30:25; Ps 36:9-10; 46:5; 65:10; 104:10.

[41]Isa 35:6-7; 41:18; 43:20; 44:3-4; 48:21; Ezek 47:1-12; Amos 9:13; Joel 4:18; Zech 14:8; Ps 107:35.

[42]G reads **šēm*, "name."

[43]As *BHS* notes, *nᵉhārîm* may well be a gloss on *yᵉʾōrîm*, for it overloads the line.

[44]Literally, "broad of hands," i.e., handbreadths. G here renders this idiom, also found in Judg 18:10; Isa 22:18; Ps 104:25; Neh 7:4; 1 Chr 4:40, with two words for broad, *platus* and *euruchoros*.

[45]See M. Dahood, *Psalms* 1 (AB 16; Garden City, New York: Doubleday, 1965) 221.

[46]See A. Negoiţă, H. Ringgren, "*Dāšan*," *TWAT* 2, 331-334.

[47]Cf. Akkadian *šamāḫu*, "grow luxuriantly." On the Hebrew root *śmḥ* see J. C. Greenfield, "Lexicographical Notes II," *HUCA* 30 (1959) 141-151.

[48]Reading **qōdeš* with the hexaplaric transliteration, Aquila and Symmachus (G. Mercati, ed., *Psalterii Hexapli Reliquiae* [Codices ex Ecclesiasticis Italiae Bibiothecis 8; Rome: Vatican Library, 1958] 77); G reads **qiddēš*.

[49]Cf. the Ugaritic use of the plural *bhtm* to denote an elaborate house.

[50]See Clifford, *Cosmic Mountain*, 158-160.

Chapter Two
WATER FROM THE MOUNTAIN

In this chapter I increase the specificity of the ideal form of the Water in the Wilderness tradition by adding the requirements that the text either refer to the time of the wandering in the desert following the Exodus or use the words *ṣûr, selaʿ* or *ḥallāmîš* to describe the source of the flow. All but one of the passages to be discussed meet both these criteria. It will be plain in most cases that this tradition is closely connected in the Israelite consciousness with fertility and apostasy.

The texts under consideration do not specify a site; all, however, refer to a rock formation, using the terms *ṣûr, selaʿ* and *ḥallāmîš*. These must be clearly defined.

Ṣûr

Ṣûr is customarily translated "rock." This is inaccurate for American English, in which "rock" is a synonym for "stone," but it is correct for British usage, in which "rock" is either a mineral or a large geological formation. British "rock" is hence equivalent to German "Fels," French "roc, rocher" and Greek *petra*. Its best English equivalent is usually mountain.

The cognates of *ṣûr* in Ugaritic (*ǵr, ẓr*)[1] and Aramaic (*ṭūr*) mean "mountain," corresponding semantically to Hebrew *har*[2]. This is clearly the sense of *ṣûr* in most biblical attestations. For example, the archaic oracle of Balaam reads, "From the peaks [*rō(')š*] of mountains (*ṣûrîm*) I see him, and from the hills [*gᵉbāʿōt*][3] I behold him" (Num 23:9). *Ṣûr* and *har* are parallel in Job 14:18: "But a mountain [*har*] falls and crumbles, and a *ṣûr* moves from its place" (cf. Job 9:5). A *ṣûr* is tall (Ps 27:5; 61:3), and, due to its crevices (Exod 33:22; Isa 2:21), it is a place of refuge (1 Sam 24:3; Isa 2:10,19,21; 17:10; Ps 27:5; 31:3; 61:3; 62:8; 71:3; 94:22; Job 24:8; 1 Chr 11:15). Yahweh (and occasionally any god) is described as a *ṣûr* (Deut 32:4,15,18,30,31,37; 1 Sam 2:2; 2 Sam 22:3,32,47; 23:3; Isa 17:10; 26:4; 30:29; Ps 18:3,32,47; 19:15; 28:1; 31:3; 62:3,7,8; 71:3; 73:26; 78:35; 89:27;

92:16; 94:22; 95:1; 144:1), in particular as a *ṣûr* of victory (*yešaʿ*/*yᵉšûʿâ*) (Deut 32:15; 2 Sam 22:47; Ps 62:3,7; 89:27; 95:1) or as the *ṣûr* of Israel (2 Sam 23:3; Isa 30:29).[4] In all these passages *ṣûr* is best translated "mountain." The use of *ṣûr* as a divine epithet is reminiscent of Mesopotamia, where a variety of gods may be called *šadû* (*KUR*) or *šadû rabû* (*KUR.GAL*), "mountain" or "great mountain."[5] The only passages which use *ṣûr* to refer to a small outcropping of rock are Judg 6:21; 13:19 and Isa 8:14 (parallel to *ʾeben*). *Ṣûr* also may denote a substance in Ps 89:44; Job 19:24; 28:10 and line 3 of the Siloam inscription (*KAI* 189), but even here references to mountains are possible.

Selaʿ

Similarly, *selaʿ* appears in parallel to *gibʿâ* (Jer 49:16), and is associated with *har* in Jer 51:25 and with both *har* and *gibʿâ* in Jer 16:16. It is tall (Isa 22:16; 33:16; Jer 49:16; 2 Chr 25:12) and ribbed with crevices (Isa 2:21; 7:19; 57:5; Jer 13:4; 16:16); it is therefore a place of refuge or secure residence (Num 24:21; Judg 20:47; 1 Sam 23:25; Isa 33:16; Jer 48:28; 49:16). Yahweh is called a *selaʿ* (2 Sam 22:2; Ps 18:3; 31:4; 42:10; 71:3). A mountain city in Edom is named *(has)selaʿ* (Judg 1:36; 2 Kgs 14:7; Isa 16:1). A smaller outcropping may occasionally be termed a *selaʿ* (Judg 6:20; Ps 137:9) or *šēn-selaʿ* (1 Sam 14:4), and *selaʿ* possibly denotes a mineral substance in Jer 5:3. The word is cognate to Arabic *salʿun*, "fissure" (<*salaʿa*, "split") and properly means either "crevice" or "crag," or, by metonymy, "mountain" (cf. *sᵉlāʿîm* in 1 Sam 13:6).

Ḥallāmîš

Ḥallāmîš occurs in Deut 8:15; 32:13; Isa 50:7; Ps 114:8 and Job 28:9. It is often translated "flint," but there is no evidence to support this interpretation. G, apparently guessing, renders *akrotomos*, "sharp," in Deut 8:15 and Job 28:9 and *stereos*, "hard," in Deut 32:13 and Isa 50:7. It is associated with the roots of mountains (Job 28:9) or with mountains themselves (Deut

8:15; 32:13; Ps 114:8). Its Akkadian cognate *elmešu/ellemešu* is a yellow gem. If the word is not Semitic, it must have been borrowed very early, before Akkadian lost its gutturals. It may, however, be derived from a root **ḥmš*, "to be hard."[6]

The texts that speak of Yahweh's having caused water or other fluids to issue from a *ṣûr, selaʿ* or *ḥallāmîš* in the time of the Israelites' desert wandering are, in approximate chronological order, Psalm 114, Deuteronomy 32, Psalm 78, Deuteronomy 8, Psalm 105 and Nehemiah 9.[7] The latter five deal with the relationship between divine beneficence and human ingratitude. As their stories of rebellion in the desert are intended to represent the contemporary backslidings of the Israelites, so the theme of sustenance in the desert by the gifts of manna, quails and especially water is symbolic of the deity's power to fertilize his holy land. The simple, mythic[8] form of the tradition is found only in Psalm 114, probably the oldest text; in the other passages it has become rigidly fixed, for sermonic purposes, to the theme of rebellion.

Psalm 114

1 When[9] Israel went forth from Egypt,[10]
The family of Jacob from a barbarous people,
2 You,[11] O Judah, became his shrine,[12]
O Israel, his kingdom.[13]
3 The Sea beheld and fled;
The Jordan turned back.
4 The mountains danced like rams,
The hills like sheep.
5 Why, O Sea, do you flee,
O Jordan, do you turn back,
6 O mountains, do you dance like rams,
O hills, like sheep?
7 Dance before the lord, O land,
Before the god of Jacob,[14]
8 Who turned the mountain [*ṣûr*] into a swamp[15] of water,
The *ḥallāmîš* into a spring of water.

The psalm displays many of the traits of early poetic Hebrew.[16] The parallelism is rigid. No colon begins with the conjunction. In v 3, the prefix conjugation (*yissōb*) is used as a preterite.[17] The -*ô* of *ma'y^enô* and the -*î* of *hahōp^ekî* (v 8) are also typical of, though not restricted to, archaic poetry.[18] *Lō'ēz* has been taken as an Aramaism and a sign of lateness,[19] but the existence of a cognate in Arabic *laǵaza* shows that the root is common Semitic, part of a large group of roots containing *lāmed* and *'ayin* (or *ǵayn*) that refer to activities of the mouth.[20]

The content of the psalm also indicates an early date. A southern provenience is suggested by the priority assigned to Judah[21] in v 2; "his shrine," ostensibly the land and people of Judah, is more likely an allusion to either Hebron[22] or Jerusalem, the principal pre- and post-Davidic cult sites of the south. The reference to Israel as "his kingdom" is less clear. Some have seen here an allusion to the northern kingdom.[23] This interpretation is unlikely, however, for in v 1 Israel clearly denotes greater Israel, the sons of Jacob. We do not expect different meanings for the same word in consecutive verses; rather, v 2 probably describes all Israel as Yahweh's kingdom, with its capital in Judah[24]. A pre-monarchic date is thus ruled out, since before David the national cult sites were in the north at Shiloh, Bethel, Shechem etc. Composition during the divided monarchy is also unlikely, since there is no evidence that the Judeans pretended that there was still one Yahwistic kingdom with its capital at Jerusalem. Only during the reigns of David and Solomon, or after 721,[25] were all the tribes united around Jerusalem.[26] The linguistic evidence favors the earlier dating.

The temporal foreshortening in the psalm is noteworthy. The unification of the tribes and the election of Judah are traced back to the entry into Canaan through the Jordan and to the Exodus itself. Since the Red Sea and Jordan are parallel, the desert vanishes for the moment, and the Israelites march from Egypt directly into Canaan. Further foreshortening occurs in vv 3-8, whose mythological resonances cannot be missed. The personified Sea/Jordan recalls Prince Sea/Judge River of Ugaritic mythology, with whom Ba'lu had struggled for dominion over the dry land[27]. The remainder of the psalm contains other, more subtle allusion to cosmogony. For example, we must examine the dancing of the mountains and the land.

In Ps 29:6, "Lebanon danced[28] like a young bull, Sirion like a bullock," the mountains dance not with joy, but with fear, upon hearing the thunder over the waters—another veiled allusion to theomachy. Apparently *rqd*, like *ḥwl*, can refer to convulsive motions of either joy or fear, both of which are typical of religious ecstasy. In Psalm 114, then, are the mountains and land dancing in fear or in joy, or both? At first glance, one would suppose the former, since the waters are said to have fled. But in the context of the cosmogonic myth, the earth should rejoice at the flight of the waters that threatened to engulf it. The positive connotations of *rqd* and *ḥwl* are confirmed by the psalm's conclusion with the bestowal of fertility—the god of Jacob possesses the power to liquefy mountains, though they be of *ḥallāmîš*. The sequence of action in vv 3-8 in fact parallels that of a creation myth—Sea/River flees, the land rejoices and is irrigated.[29] In other words, Yahweh both turns the wet to dry (vv 3, 5) and the dry to wet (v 8), a parallelism we will encounter again. The use of language reminiscent of creation is another argument against seeing the division of the kingdoms in v 2; would a Judean ascribe such antiquity to the bifurcation of the people?

Ps 114:8 gives no reason for the conversion of the mountain to a swamp; i.e., it contains no thirst tradition. It simply associates this act with Creation, Exodus and Occupation, suggesting it is of comparable significance.

Deuteronomy 32

Deuteronomy 32, the Song of Moses, gives us more information about the liquefication of the mountain. The date of this work is controverted.[30] The passage contains no historical allusions, and some of the archaic features of its language may be discounted as pseudo-archaisms, yet the extensive contacts with 1 Sam 2:1-10 and 2 Samuel 22=Psalm 18 corroborate the linguistic arguments for a dating in the early divided monarchy,[31] while connections to northern prophets, especially Hosea,[32] and to D and Dtr forbid too late a date. On the whole, the ninth century is most likely.

The opening invocation is reminiscent of prophetic rebuke: "Listen, O Heavens...hear, O Earth" (Deut 32:1).[33] After a preliminary admonition in the sapiential vein, the poet refers his foolish and immoral listeners to days of old, early in the history of humanity:

*6b*Is he [Yahweh] not your father who begot you,
Who made and created you?
*7*Remember the primordial days;
Recall the years of the infinite past.
Ask your father—he will tell you—
Your elders—they will inform you.
*8*When Elyon distributed land to the nations,
When he divided the sons of Man,
He erected the boundaries of the peoples
According to the number of the gods.[34]
*9*But Yahweh's own share was Jacob;[35]
Israel was the land of his fief.
*10*He found him in a land of desert,
In a chaotic, screaming[36] waste.
He enveloped him; he kept watch over him;
He guarded him like the pupil of his eye.
*11*As an eagle[37] watches[38] his nest
And hovers[39] over his chicks,
So did he spread his wings and take him;
He bore him upon his pinion.
*12*Yahweh alone led him;
There was no foreign god beside him.
*13*He led him up[40] the heights of the land,[41]
And he ate[42] the produce of the field.[43]
He suckled him with honey[44] from the crag [*selaʿ*]
And oil from the *ḥallāmîš* of the mountain [*ṣûr*],
*14*Curds of bullocks and milk of sheep,[45]
With the fat of rams and of mountain goats[46]
All from Bashan,[47] and of billy goats,
With the fattest[48] of wheat,
And the blood of the grape[49] you drank as wine.[50]

As in Psalm 114, the formation of the people is associated with the events of Creation; the name Elyon seems originally to have been an epithet of the deity as Creator or primordial Progenitor.[51] The use of *tōhû* is therefore not accidental. The state of Israel in the desert is equivalent to that of the earth before the intervention of Yahweh (cf. Gen 1:2).

In Deuteronomy 32, as in Psalm 114, the goal of the journey is not the mountain of lawgiving but a mountain flowing with fertility, here in the form of honey, oil, curds, fat, wheat and wine. The prose summary (Deut 31:16-21) correctly perceives this language to be a more detailed variant of the familiar description of a fertile country as "flowing with milk and honey" (Deut 31:20), the symbols *par excellence* of agricultural and pastoral fertility.[52] The description of the source of the fluids as *sela'...ḥalmîš ṣûr* also serves to associate this fertility with the motif of Water in the Wilderness.

The image of a land flowing with such fluids has a long history, extending from Bronze Age mythology through medieval Cockaigne to the "Big Rock Candy Mountain" of American folksong.[53] At Ugarit, the bath water of the goddess 'Anatu consists of *ṭl šmm šmn 'arṣ/rbb rkb 'rpt/ṭl šmm tskh/rbb nskh kbkbm,* "Dew of the heavens, fat of the land,/Shower of the Cloudrider,/Dew the sky pours/Shower the stars pour,"[54] which is echoed in the description of fertility found in Isaac's blessings.[55] A more famous example from Ugarit is 'Ilu's dream of the resurrection of Ba'lu, in which *šmm šmn tmṭrn/nḫlm tlk nbt,* "the heavens rained oil/The wadis ran with honey."[56]

Ps 36:9 uses this imagery to describe Zion as the source of fertilizing waters: "They are refreshed from the sap/fat (*dešen*) of your house, and you give them drink from your fertilizing brook." Joel 4:18 also associates waters flowing from the temple and the fertility of Palestine:

> On that day
> The mountains will drip juice,
> And the hills will run with milk,
> And all the channels of Judah will run with water,
> And a spring will arise in the house of Yahweh
> And water the wadi of Shittim.

A possible addendum[57] to Amos cleverly de-mythologizes the ancient image by inserting human intermediaries (9:13).

> Behold, days are coming—word of Yahweh—
> When the plowman will overtake the reaper,

And the grape-treader him who plants,[58]
And the mountains will drip juice,
And all the hills will melt.

The poet has, in effect, heightened the hyperbole of Lev 26:5, "Your threshing will overtake the vintage, and the vintage will overtake the sowing." These biblical parallels show that, while the designations *ṣûr, selaʿ* and *ḥallāmîš* are appropriate to the water-giving mountain in the desert, this *ṣûr* is also the land of Canaan. The remainder of the Song of Moses, dealing with Israel's infidelity and Yahweh's punishment and relenting, also fits the setting in the land.

<Jacob ate and was full;>[59]
15 Jeshurun grew fat and kicked.
You grew fat, you grew thick, you were gorged.
He forsook Eloah who had made him,
And he denigrated the mountain of his victory.
16 They made him jealous with strange ones,
With abominations they provoked him.
17 They sacrificed to spirits, not to Eloah,
Gods with whom they were unacquainted,
New ones from nearby,
Whom your fathers never had known.[60]
18 You forgot the mountain that begot you.[61]
Weren't mindful of the god who gave you birth.

As a punishment, the aggrieved deity brings against Israel a foreign nation which almost exterminates it, but which in the end is itself put down for excessive pride. The Song ends cheerily with the slaughter of the foe and the pardon of the people. We note a sequence of divine grace, human sin, divine vengeance, human atonement, divine forgiveness, but our concern is with the first two steps—the gift of fertility followed by disobedience, here apostasy.

Psalm 78

As noted above, scholars have attempted to read many historical situations into the Song of Moses. The first recorded such effort may be Psalm 78, probably written during the reign of Hezekiah.[62] Both works follow the prophetic-deuteronomic-deuteronomistic view of Israelite history.

The poems share more than this. They each begin with an exhortation to listen in the wisdom style (Deut 32:1-3; Ps 78:1-22); both stress father-to-son transmission of historical memory (Deut 32:7; Ps 78:3-6). At this point the works part company, in accordance with their respective functions. Deuteronomy 32 is an ambiguous, almost Delphic oracle, while Psalm 78 shows how the older poem's threats and promises of aid had been realized for Ephraim and Judah. Accordingly, Deuteronomy 32 and Psalm 78 differ in their presentations of history.

The Song of Moses speaks simply of a journey from a desert to a mountain of fertility that proves to be Canaan itself, where the gluttonous people turn against Yahweh and worship other gods. Psalm 78 restores the depth of history by telling of two journeys, one from the parted sea through the desert to a mountain that yields water, whereat the people rebel (vv 12-33), and the other from Egypt to Canaan, "his holy mountain, the mountain his right hand had acquired" (vv 42-72).[63] But here, too, they rebel. In these latter verses, the events of the desert are skipped, so that there is virtually no overlap between the two sections. Chronologically, the second recitation encompasses the first.

The double structure of the historical section of Psalm 78 is confusing, yet there does seem to be a sequence of thought and a unifying theme of forgetfulness. The eighth century Ephraimites are defeated (v 9) because they have not obeyed the covenant (v 10), since they do not remember the deity's miraculous sustenance of Israel in the desert (vv 11-17). They should learn from the example of the generation of Egypt, who themselves doubted Yahweh's power and were punished (vv 18-33), though their requests for food and drink were granted, presumably lest Yahweh's reputation suffer. Yet that generation did not learn the lesson, but continually rebelled (vv 34-41), even though they had seen the plagues of Egypt (vv 42-51).[64] The Ephraimites should consider also the generation that entered the land, who forgot all the above and were punished with the loss of Yahweh's ark, the symbol of his presence (vv 52-64).[65] Though these were the sins of all Israel, Ephraim suffered in particular, since divine favor was restored to Judah, while Ephraim, for no given reason, remained rejected.[66] Perhaps the psalmist implies that Yahweh already knew that the Ephraimites would not merit his presence. The psalm ends with the election of Judah, Zion and David. It is a propaganda piece encouraging the northern kingdom, or at least its defectors, to return to Davidic rule.

For our purposes, the most important aspect of the double presentation of history is that the two narratives are parallel, in that both tell of a journey to a mountain. At each mountain the people rebel and are punished. At the mountain of Yahweh (=Canaan) the sin is idolatry (v 58), while at the desert mountain the sin is greed (vv 15-20).

> *15* He cleft a mountain [**ṣûr*][67] in the desert
> And watered[68] with[69] the great deep [*t^{e}hôm*[70] *rabbâ*]
> *16* He brought forth streams from a crag [*selaʿ*]
> And brought down water like rivers [*n^{e}hārôt*].
> *17* But they sinned further against him
> By rebelling[71] against Elyon in the waste,
> *18* And they tested God in their heart
> By seeking food for their throat.
> *19* Thus they spoke against God:
> "Can God set a table in the desert?
> *20* Granted that he struck a mountain so that water flowed,
> Drenching[72] the wadis,
> Can he also give bread?
> Can he provide meat for his people?"

Yahweh proceeds to rain down food.[73] While in Deuteronomy 32 the mountain flows with food and drink and is equivalent to Canaan, here the mountain is distinct from Canaan and its flow is of water, while food falls as rain. Note that this water is not described as a small pool for drinking, but as the great deep, as rivers that drench the ravines. The act of cleaving the sea (v 13) is parallel to the cleaving of the mountain in v 15,[74] a contrast of turning wet to dry and dry to wet that we noted in Psalm 114 and will see again. The poetic hyperbole "deep(s)...rivers" evokes cosmology, and in particular it recalls the abode of 'Ilu, perhaps intentionally, given the parallelism of this mountain with the holy mountain of v 54.

Deuteronomy 8

This deuteronomic sermon[75] also mentions the water in the desert. Here, too, the motif is associated with the fertility of Canaan and (in the later redaction) with the complacent apostasy of the people. The entire chapter is worth quoting, as it is the fullest exposition of the significance of the theme of sustenance in the wilderness.

> *1*Observe and perform all of the commandment[76] I command you this day, so that you will live and multiply and arrive and possess the land which Yahweh[77] promised to your fathers. *2*Remember the entire journey on which Yahweh, your god, has led you for forty years[78] in the desert, in order to afflict and test you, to know what is in your heart, whether or not you will obey his commandments. *3*He has afflicted you and made you hungry and fed you manna, which neither you[79] nor your fathers knew, in order to show you that not by bread alone does man live, but rather man lives by the utterance of Yahweh's mouth. *4*Your robe[80] has not worn out nor your foot[81] swollen for forty years. *5*You know in your heart that, as a man chastises his son, so Yahweh chastises you. *6*Observe all the commandments of Yahweh by walking in his way and fearing him. *7*For Yahweh, your god, is bringing you to a good land,[82] a land[83] of running brooks and springs of the deeps[84] emerging in valley and highland, *8*a land of wheat and barley and vine and fig and[85] pomegranate, a land of oleagenous olive and honey, *9*a land in which you will not eat bread in poverty, in[86] which you will not lack anything, a land whose stones are iron and from whose mountains you may mine copper. *10*You will eat and be sated and bless Yahweh, your god, for the good land which he will have given you. *11*Beware lest you forget Yahweh, your god, by not observing his commandments and laws and statutes which I have commanded

> you today. *12*(Beware) lest you eat and be sated, and
> you build good houses and settle down,[87] *13*and[88]
> your cattle and flocks increase,[89] and you acquire
> much silver and gold, and all your property
> increase,[89] *14*and your heart grow haughty and you
> forget Yahweh, your god, who brought you forth from
> the land of Egypt, from slave quarters, *15*who led you
> in the[90] great and terrible desert (amid) *sārāp*-snake[91]
> and scorpion, a thirsty place where there was no
> water, who produced for you water from the mountain
> [*ṣûr*] of *ḥallāmîš*, *16*who fed you manna in the desert,
> which your fathers had not known, in order to test
> and afflict you, in order to improve you for the future,
> *17*and (beware lest) you say in your[92] heart, "my
> power and the strength of my hand has done this great
> deed." *18*Remember Yahweh, your god—that it was
> he who gave you power to do great deeds in order[93] to
> fulfill his covenant which he[94] swore to your fathers
> (and which is still valid) as of today. *19*[Dtr^2:]Now if
> you forget Yahweh, your god, and go after other gods
> and worship them and sacrifice to them, I warn[95] you
> today that you will surely perish. *20*Just like the
> nations that Yahweh is going to destroy before you, so
> you will perish, since you will not have heeded the
> voice of Yahweh, your god.

This text interprets Yahweh's miraculous sustenance of Israel in the desert as a foreshadowing of the bounty they may expect in the land. In the original text ending in v 18, the sin that ensues is arrogant self-reliance, as opposed to reliance upon Yahweh, but in the Exilic version the sin is apostasy, as in the texts we have already examined.

Nevertheless, the Josianic version also saw the self-reliance culminating in apostasy, for the sermon extends through chapter 11. Chapter 9, by rehearsing past infidelities to Yahweh, shows that these are considered foreshadowings of infidelity in the land. The first part of chapter 10 tells that Yahweh forgave the wilderness generation, the implication being that pardon is also available to their descendants. Further exhortation about pleasing Yahweh follows. Chapter eleven opens describing more of the kindnesses that Yahweh has performed for Israel, up through the possession of the land. Then this warning:

> 13 If you heed the[96] commandments I am issuing to
> you today by loving Yahweh, your god, with all
> your[97] heart and all your[97] soul, 14 then I[98] will
> grant the rain of your land[99] in its proper time, the
> former and latter rains, that you may gather your
> grain, wine and oil, 15 and I[100] will put grass in
> your[101] field for your cattle, that you may eat and be
> sated. 16 Beware[102] lest your[103] heart be seduced and
> you turn aside and worship other gods and bow to
> them. 17 Then the anger of Yahweh will be kindled
> against you, and he will shut the heavens so that there
> not be rain, and the earth not yield its crop, so that
> you perish quickly from the good land which Yahweh
> is about to give[103] you (Deut 11:13-17).

Hence, the association of fertility and apostasy is made explicit in the pre-exilic text as well.

Psalm 105

The next text in this group is Psalm 105, which alludes only to the beneficence of Yahweh. The themes of rebellion and punishment are not absent, however. Psalm 105 is the first panel of a triptych comprised of Psalms 105-107.[104] The first psalm recounts Yahweh's gracious acts, the second the rebellions of the Israelites and the punishments they incurred, while Psalm 107 tells of Yahweh's relenting and returning his people from exile. The author of these three poems of the early post-exilic period[105] has simply reorganized the classical pattern of grace, rebellion, punishment, forgiveness.

Psalm 105 tells of Yahweh's acts of kindness from patriarchal times up through the Conquest. It omits the crossing of the Red Sea, but this is covered in Ps 106:9-12. Just prior to the occupation of the land is mention of food and water in the desert.

> 40 They[106] requested, and he brought[107] quail
> And sated them with the bread of heaven.
> 41 He opened a mountain [*ṣûr*] and water flowed;
> It went as a river[108] in the arid wastes.
> 42 For he remembered his holy word

Feature	Ps 105	Ps 106	Ps 107
hal(ᵉ)lû-yâ	[1]	1	1
hôdû lᵉ yahwe(h)	1	1	1(8,15,21,31)
kî ṭôb kî lᵉ ʿôlam ḥasdô		1	1
Proclamation	1-2	2	2
zkr	5,8	4,7	
niplāʾōt	5	7	8,15,21,24,31
hôdîaʿ	1	8	
hithallēl	3	5	
Miṣrayim... ʾereṣ Ḥām	23	21-22	
Miracles in land of Ham	27	22	
bāḥîr/bāḥar	6,26,43	5,23	
baśśar lāhem		44	6,13,19,28
hiśbîaʿ	40		9
Water in *ṣiyyâ*	41		35
Food in desert	40	14-15	9
Water into *midbār*		9	33
marâ/himrâ	28	7,43	11
qibbēṣ		47	3
ṣār (enemy)	24		2
Moses and Aaron	26	16	
Imprisonment in *barzel*	18		10, (14), 16
Desert parallel to Exile		26-27	3-4
naḥalâ	11	5	
nikna'/hiknîaʿ		42	12
kāšal	37		12

To Abraham his servant,
43 And he brought out his people in joy,
In song his elect,
44 And he gave them the lands of nations,
And they inherited the fruit of the labor of countries,
45 So that they would observe his statutes
And obey his laws (Ps 105:40-45).

As in Psalm 78, the flow is compared to a river. It is apparently regarded as the culmination of the desert period, and is described as impinging upon the occupation of the land.

Nehemiah 9

The final text that meets both the added parameters of this chapter is Nehemiah 9:6-37. Like Psalms 78 and 105-106, it is a recitation of the history of the relationship between Yahweh and Israel emphasizing repeatedly the infidelity of the latter and the graciousness of the former. The style is not poetic, yet the words fall into natural strophae. Vv 7-12 record the kindnesses of Yahweh from Ur to Sinai. Then

13 On Mount Sinai you descended
And spoke with them from heaven
And gave them just laws
And true statutes
And good ordinances and commandments.
14 And your holy Sabbath
You made known to them
And commandments and ordinances,
And you commanded the Torah to them
Through Moses your slave.
15 You gave them bread from the sky for their hunger
And you produced water from a crag [*sela'*] for their thirst.
And you told them to come to inherit the land
Which you swore[109] to give to them.
16 But they and their fathers were insubordinate
And stiffened their neck
And did not heed you commandments.
17 They refused to listen

And did not recall your wonders
Which you did for them.
They stiffened their neck
And rebelliously tried[110] to return to their servitude in Egypt.[111]
But you are the god of pardon,[112]
Merciful and compassionate,
Patient and greatly faithful—[113]
You did not desert them.
*18*Even when they made for themselves a molten calf
And said, "This is your god[114]
Who took you[115] from Egypt"
And committed great acts of contempt.

Note the association of manna, water and Canaan, also connected in Ps 105:40-44. The text goes on to say that Yahweh did not abandon the Israelites, but sustained them with manna and water (v 20) and led them to Canaan. There

*25*They took fortified cities and the fat land;
They inherited houses full of all good things,
Hewn cisterns, vineyards and olives,
Many[116] fruit trees.
They ate, became sated and grew fat,
Delighting in your great goodness.
*26*They mutinied[117] and rebelled against you;
They cast your Torah behind their back;
They killed your prophets,
Who warned them in order to return them to you,
And committed great acts of contempt.

Once again, fertility and prosperity are followed by rebellion, described in phraseology influenced by Deut 6:11; 8:7-13; 32:15 and many other biblical texts.[118] As in Psalm 78, we find a parallelism inherent in the structure—the first act of rebellion is the worship of the calf at Sinai, despite the gifts of manna and water; the second act of rebellion, more generally described, also derives from the complacency engendered by prosperity. This relation between prosperity, rebellion, punishment and forgiveness is the poet's theme; he sees himself in the third stage of the cycle.

Job 28:9-11

There remains one text which meets only one of our criteria. This is Job 28:9-11, which begins with a description of mining operations:

> *9* He [the miner] sends his hand into the *ḥallāmîš*,
> He turns over mountains at the root.[119]
> *10* In the mountains [*ṣûrôt*] he cleaves channels,[120]
> And his eye sees every precious thing.
> *11* He seeks the sources of the rivers[121]
> And brings the hidden to light.

In describing a miner's journey to the depths of the earth, the author of Job[122] characteristically delights in allusive language. At times it is apposite, as in the reference to the "sources of the rivers"; at other times, as in the mention of *ḥallāmîš* and of *y*^{e}*'ōrîm* cleaving *ṣûrôt*, it seems gratuitous. That is, the similarity to the Water in the Wilderness tradition is a result of verbal artifice, and no light is shed upon the object of our inquiry.

Summary

This chapter examined the close relation between fertility and rebellion, particularly apostasy, in various biblical texts; we saw that Water in the Wilderness is often connected with some or all of these themes. Psalm 114 alludes only to fertility, but Deuteronomy 8-11, 32 clearly associate the Water in the Wilderness with fertility and apostasy. In Psalm 78 the structure of the psalm suggests a parallelism between fertility and apostasy in the land, on the one hand, and water and ingratitude in the desert, on the other, but the association is far more subtly conveyed than in the Deuteronomic texts. Still more subtle is Psalm 105, which alludes to Water in the Wilderness only, if at all, in the sequential remembrance of the production of water and the gift of the land. The connection to rebellion and apostasy is to be found only within the larger framework of Psalms 105-106. In Nehemiah 9, the Israelites rebel subsequent to the production of water, again mentioned in association with Canaan, yet there is no apostasy, but rather an attempt to return to Egypt. Except for Psalm 114, all these texts mention both water and food (manna and/or quails), the point being that Yahweh is able to provide the bounty typical of Canaan even in the desert. The rebellion motif is worthy of study in its own right, and the following chapter is devoted to it; for the present, I wish simply to observe that just as rebellion in the desert prefigures rebellion in the land, so water in the desert prefigures fertility in the land.

[1]On Ugaritic *ǵayn*, see J. Blau ("On Problems of Polyphony and Archaism in Ugaritic Spelling," *JAOS* 88 [1968] 523-526) and W. von Soden ("Kleine Beiträge zum Ugaritischen und Hebräischen," *Hebräische Wortforschung* [Fs. W. Baumgartner; VTSup 16; Leiden: Brill, 1967] 291-294). Ugaritic orthography is surprisingly consistent in its choice of *ǵ* or *ẓ* for individual words, the only fluctuating lexemes being *ẓm'/ǵm'*, "to thirst" and *ẓr/ǵr*, "mountain"; see Y. Avishur, "The Ghost-expelling Incantation from Ugarit (Ras Ibn Ḥani 78/20)," *UF* 13 (1981) 18-19.

[2]The common derivation of *ṣûr, ǵr/ẓr* and *ṭûr* is unconvincingly denied by O. Rössler, "Ghain im Ugaritischen," *ZA* 54 (1961) 158-172.

[3]The traditional translation of *gib'â* as "hill" is maintained here as an unfortunate consequence of the lack of a suitable synonym for "mountain"; there is in fact no evidence that a *gib'â* is lower than a *har*.

[4]Cf. the PNN *Ṣûr* (Num 25:15), *'Ĕlîṣûr* (Num 1:5; 2:10; 7:30,35; 10:18), *Ṣûrîšadday* (Num 1:6 etc.), *P*^{e}*dâṣûr* (Num 1:10 etc.) and *Ṣûrî'ēl* (Num 3:35), the Mari names given in H. B. Huffmon, *Amorite Personal Names in the Mari Texts* (Baltimore: Hopkins, 1965) 258 and the Ugaritic names cited in F. Grondahl, *Die Personennamen der Texte aus Ugarit* (Studia Pohl 1; Rome: PBI, 1967) 141.

[5]K. L. Tallqvist, *Akkadische Götterepitheta* (StudOr 7; Helsinki: Societas Orientalis Fennica, 1938) 221.

[6]See von Soden, "Kleine Beiträge," 297-300.

[7]Omitting the Massah-Meribah accounts, to be examined below in chapter three.

[8]Mythic in two senses—first, in that the actors in Ps 114:3-8 are Yahweh and nature personified, without humans, and second, in that these verses function as an assurance of the dominion of the deity over Nature and his ability to provide water, just as the Ugaritic myth of the death and resurrection of Ba'lu assures the reader of the power of the storm god to return from death (the drought period) and restore fertility.

[9]In the G the psalm begins "Hallelujah." In the MT this is the conclusion of Psalm 113.

[10]The G's *laou barbarou* is apt, as is "barbarous" in English, because the psalmist's intent is not just to note that the Egyptians did not speak Hebrew. The Israelite attitude toward speakers of foreign tongues is one of mingled hostility and fear (Deut 28:49; Isa 18:2,7; 33:19; Jer 5:15 and Ezek 3:5-6); note that according to

Israelite legend (Genesis 11), human sin was the origin of diversity of languages. Ps 81:6 (see p. 78, n. 64) also refers to the unintelligibility of Egyptian in the context of the Exodus. On expressions for "to speak a foreign tongue" in various ancient languages see Tigay, "'Heavy of Mouth' and 'Heavy of Tongue': On Moses' Speech Difficulty," ***BASOR*** 231 (1978) 58 and add the Modern English correspondent to Greek *barbaros*, Sanskrit *barbara-*, Latin *balbus*: "blah-blah-blah."

[11] *Y^{e}hûdâ*, as a tribal name, is properly masculine. After the division of the kingdom it came to be a national name, hence sometimes feminine (Jer 3:6-11; 13:19; 14:2; 23:6; 33:16; Joel 4:20; Zech 14:14; Lam 1:3). Since the psalm probably dates to the United Monarchy, I suppose an ambiguous *hyt*, intended to be second person masculine singular (for lack of internal *mater lectionis* in this period, cf. the defective spelling of *Dāwīd* in Samuel and Kings), was read as a third feminine singular (cf. *hyt* in line 3 of the Siloam inscription [*KAI* 189]). The psalmist may address his audience directly, just as he addresses the Jordan, mountains and possibly the earth.

[12] In Jer 2:3 Israel is also called Yahweh's *qōdeš*, but the parallel with *rē(')šît t^{e}bû'ātōh* shows that there *qōdeš* is a vegetable offering, something set apart. In Ps 114:2, however, *qōdeš*, parallel to *memšālâ*, should refer to a shrine. M. Dahood (*Psalms* 3 [AB; Garden City, New York: Doubleday, 1970] 134-135) compares *CTA* 3.3.27, 6.64, *bqdš bǵr nḥlty bn'm bgb' tl'iyt*, "in the holy mountain of my fief, in my fair hill of my might"; on the hendiadys see Cross, *Canaanite Myth*, 156, n. 46. It is less likely, however, due to their distance, that in Ps 114:2 we should treat *qodšô...mamš^{e}lôtāw* as a hendiadys.

[13] This use of the plural is probably analogous to that attested for architectural complexes; cf. Ugaritic *bhtm*.

[14] V 7 is ambiguous and may also be translated "Dance before the lord, O nation,/Before God, O Jacob" (cf. "family of Jacob" in v 1).

[15] An *'ăgam* is apparently a reedy pool or swamp; cf. Exod 7:19; 8:1; Isa 14:23; 41:18; Jer 51:32; Ps 107:35. Other derivatives of the root are *'agmôn*, "reed," Syriac *'egmā'*, Arabic *'ajamatun* and Akkadian *agammu*, all denoting a marshy jungle.

[16] See D. A. Robertson, *Linguistic Evidence in Dating Early Hebrew Poetry* (SBL Dissertation 3; Missoula, Montana: Scholars Press, 1972) and F. M. Cross, Jr., and D. N. Freedman, *Studies in Ancient Yahwistic Poetry* (SBL Dissertation 21; Hopkins diss., 1950; Missoula, Montana: Scholars Press, 1975).

[17] Cross (*Canaanite Myth*, 139) has prefix conjugation preterites in v 5 (*tanûs, tissōb*) and v 6 (*tirq^{e}dû*), because he translates these verbs

in the past tense. The Hebrew is ambiguous, but I believe the present tense is more appropriate to the liturgical setting.

[18]See Robertson, *Linguistic Evidence*, 69-77.

[19]C. A. Briggs and E. G. Briggs, *A Critical and Exegetical Commentary on the Book of Psalms* 2 (2 vols.; ICC; Edinburgh: Clark, 1906) 390. The psalm is also considered exilic or post-exilic by A. F. Kirkpatrick, *The Book of Psalms* 3 (3 vols.; Cambridge Bible for Schools and Colleges; Cambridge: University, 1901) 680; E. J. Kissane, *The Book of Psalms* 2 (2 vols.; Westminster: Newman, 1953) 204 and W. O. E. Oesterly, *The Psalms* 2 (2 vols.; London: Society for Promoting Christian Knowledge, 1939) 470.

[20]The Hebrew examples are *lw'/l'*, "swallow, talk wildly," which produces *lōa'*, "throat"; *l'b*, "jest"; *l'g*, "mock"; *l'ṭ*, "swallow," *'lg*, "stammer"; *bl'*, "swallow"; *'ls/ṣ/z*, "exult"; *m^{e}tall^e'ôt*, "teeth."

[21]In Ps 114:2 Judah and Israel are at the same time groups of people departing from Egypt and sovereign entities settled in the land.

[22]Both the patricarchal legends and the specific notice in 2 Sam 15:7-8 show that Hebron was the cultic center of Judah.

[23]Gunkel, *Die Psalmen* (Göttingen: Vandenhoeck & Ruprecht, 1929) 494; A. Weiser, *Die Psalmen* (ATD 14/15; Göttingen: Vandenhoeck & Ruprecht, 1966) 488.

[24]Exod 19:3-6, especially v 6, "you will be my royalty of priests and my holy nation," is often invoked as a parallel text which pairs cult and sovereignty. *Mamleket kōhănîm* is within *gôy qādôš* (see W. L. Moran, "A Kingdom of Priests," *The Bible in Modern Catholic Thought* [ed. J. L. McKenzie; New York: Herder and Herder, 1962] 7-20), just as in Ps 114:2 the shrine of Judah is within the kingdom of Israel.

[25]So C. Stuhlmueller, *Psalms* 2 (Old Testament Message 22; Wilmington, Delaware: Glazier, 1983) 137. R. Kittel (*Die Psalmen* [KAT; Leipzig: Deichert, 1914] 406) also dates the psalm to pre-exilic Judah.

[26]Cross (*Canaanite Myth*, 103-105, 138-139) sees Psalm 114 as originating in the pre-monarchical cult of Gilgal. If this is so, the psalm's current Judahite stance must be due to revision; in v 2 another name for Israel such as Jeshurun was replaced by Judah. Kraus (*Psalmen* 2 [BKAT; Neukirchen: Neukirchener Verlag, 1960] 781) more persuasively sees it as a later Judahite text deriving from the traditions of pre-monarchic Gilgal.

[27]The following are the Ugaritic and biblical combat myth texts: Ba'lu defeats Sea/River in *CTA* 2.4.11-27; 'Anatu kills Sea/River and muzzles the *tunnānu*-dragon, the twisting serpent and seven-headed *Šlyṭ*, among other foes (*CTA* 3.3.35-39). According to *PRU* II.3.3-11, she bound the dragon. An unspecified person,

most likely Ba'lu, is said to have smitten Lôtānu (Heb. *Liwyātān*), the twisting serpent and seven-headed *Šlyṭ* (*CTA* 5.1.1-3,27-30). Yahweh limits the Sea in Jer 5:22; Prov 8:27-29. Conflict between Yahweh and the waters is implied in 2 Sam 22 (=Ps 18):16; Isa 11:15; 50:2; Nah 1:4; Ps 29:3; 93:1-4. Yahweh battles Rahab/Sea in Ps 89:10-11; Job 9:13; 26:12-13. The enemy is Leviathan in Ps 74:13-15, the dragon (*tannîn*) in Job 7:12. In Isa 41:5; Hab 3:10; Ps 77:17; 104:7 the flight of the waters is a way of describing the creation of dry land.

28 Reading **wayyirqōd-m* (enclitic *mēm*) with H. L. Ginsberg, *Kitbê 'Ûgārît* (Jerusalem: Bialik, 1936) 130.

29 Note that *ḥûlî* might also be translated "writhe in childbirth," again alluding to fertility.

30 The *terminus ad quem* for the piece is ca. 550, when Dtr^2 inserted the Song of Moses at the end of Deuteronomy; see R. E. Friedman, *The Exile and Biblical Narrative* (HSM 22; Chico, California: Scholars Press, 1981) 13-16. I cannot accept the arguments for a later date by E. Sellin, "Wann wurde das Moselied Dtn 32 gedichtet?" *ZAW* 43 (1925) 161-173 and R. Meyer, "Die Bedeutung von Deuteronomium 32, 8f. 43 (4Q) für die Auslegung des Moseliedes," *Verbannung und Heimkehr* (Fs. W. Rudolph; ed. A. Kuschke; Tübingen: Mohr [Siebeck], 1961) 197-209. The earliest date tolerated by the linguistic evidence is the eleventh century (Robertson, *Linguistic Evidence*, 146, 155). Albright ("Some Remarks on the Song of Moses in Deuteronomy XXXII," *VT* 9 [1959] 339-346) assigns the Song to the eleventh century, chiefly for linguistic, orthographic and prosodic reasons. O. Eissfeldt (*Das Lied Moses Deuteronomium 32 1-43 und das Lehrgedicht Asaphs Psalm 78 samt einer Analyse der Umgebung des Mose-Liedes* [Sachsische Akademie, philologisch-historische Klasse 104:5; Berlin: Akademie, 1958]) also dates it to the eleventh century because of supposed allusions to the Philistine wars. On pp. 15-21 Eissfeldt gives a survey of older scholarship, some of which considers the work post-exilic, also because of putative historical references. This method must be abandoned. The Song of Moses consciously avoids specific references, because it is an oracle of threat and consolation intended to be applicable to any situation. Wright ("Lawsuit,") argues that affinities with northern prophecy and the deuteronomistic writers indicate a date between 900 and 600, preferably in the late ninth century (pp. 66-67). G. E. Mendenhall ("Samuel's 'Broken *Rib*': Deuteronomy 32," *No Famine in the Land* (Fs. J. McKenzie; ed. J. W. Flanagan, A. W. Robinson [Missoula, Montana: Scholars Press, 1975] 63-74) responds that Deuteronomy 32 is not just typical of prophetic and

deuteronomistic thought, it is *proto*typical, and its author is Samuel. Mendenhall is right that we cannot rule out a pre-ninth century date for lack of comparable material, but his acceptance of Eissfeldt's views makes his own position unconvincing. Freedman's typology of divine epithets dates the Song in the tenth or early ninth century; see "Divine Names and Titles in Early Hebrew Poetry," *Magnalia Dei* (Fs. G. E. Wright; eds. F. M. Cross, W. E. Lemke and P. D. Miller; Garden City, New York: Doubleday, 1976) 77-80. On the compositional scheme see P. W. Skehan, "The Structure of the Song of Moses in Deuteronomy (Deut. 32:1-43)" *CBQ* 13 (1951) 153-163.

[31]Freedman ("Psalm 113 and the Song of Hannah," *Pottery, Poetry, and Prophecy* [Winona Lake, Indiana: Eisenbrauns, 1980] 243) dates 1 Sam 2:1-10 to the tenth century "or possibly later." Cross and Freedman (*Yahwistic Poetry,* 125-158) date 2 Samuel 22=Psalm 18 to the tenth to eighth century and ascribe it a northern provenance. By Robertson's analysis (*Linguistic Evidence,* 139, 155) the psalm falls into the eleventh-tenth centuries. His chronology ought to be lowered, however, since he dates his yardstick, Psalm 78, to the tenth or ninth century (p. 155), whereas more likely it dates to the late eighth century (see below, p. 46, n. 62).

One of the most characteristic features of the Song of Moses is its use of *ṣûr* as a virtual synonym for *'ēl,* "god" (vv 4,15,30,31,37). Compare 1 Sam 2:2 and 2 Sam 22(Ps 18):3 with Deut 32:31 and 2 Sam 22:3 (Psalm 18:2) with Deut 32:37 (*ṣûr* is also used in 2 Sam 22[Ps 18]:47 as a divine epithet). Compare, too, 1 Sam 2:6 with Deut 32:39 and note the association of the roots *'qš* and *ptl* in 2 Sam 22(Ps 18):27 and in Deut 32:25. Also note the phrase "foundations of mountains" in Ps 18:8 and in Deut 32:22. These are features shared *uniquely* by these poems. Other connections, such as *'Elyôn* and *bămotê,* are attested elsewhere and so are less valuable for dating. If some individual phrases are paralleled in early texts (compare Deut 32:14 and Gen 49:11), others are found in later passages (compare Deut 32:25 and Lam 1:20).

[32]Hosea displays affinities with the Song of Moses in Hos 1:9, where *lō(') 'ammî* and *lō(')- 'ehye(h) lākem* echo Deut 32:21; in Hos 2:12, where *nablûtāh* recalls Deut 32:6, and in Hos 2:16-25, where Yahweh leads Israel into the desert and makes the wilderness bloom (in v 17, *petaḥ tiqwâ* may be an irrigation system; cf. *miqwe(h)* in Gen 1:10; Exod 7:19; Lev 11:36). Hos 5:14 resembles Deut 32:39, while 9:10 agrees with Deut 32:10 that Yahweh found Israel in the desert. Hos 11:1-2, like Deut 32:6, stresses the

fatherhood of Yahweh, and both Hos 11:8 and Deut 32:32 refer to the Cities of the Plain. Finally, Hos 13:5-8 presents the sequence desert wandering, satiety, forgetfulness, punishment. While most of these items are present elsewhere (for instance, Isa 43:11-13 echoes Hos 5:14 and Deut 32:39), their clustering in Hosea may be significant.

33 For the role of nature, cf. Isa 1:2; Jer 2:12; Mic 6:2; Ps 50:4; Job 20:27.

34 Reading **hā'ělōhîm* for MT *Yiśrā'ēl* with G and 4QDt; P. W. Skehan ("Qumran and the Present State of Old Testament Studies: the Masoretic Text," *JBL* 78 [1959] 21) omits the definite article, but F. M. Cross tells me it is definitely present. *B^e^nê 'ělōhîm*, here taken as analogous to *b^e^nê hann^e^bî'îm* etc., may also be translated "sons of God"; cf. Ugaritic *bn 'ilm* as an epithet of Death in *CTA* 4-6; *Ug5* 4.14, which probably, as a singular, is to be understood as "son of 'Ilu" plus the enclitic, although we do get *ben* with a plural noun in Ps 29:6 (here the enclitic is also possible); Neh 3:8 and Esth 8:10. Other attestations of the phrase that are, like Deut 32:8, ambiguous, are *KAI* 26.A.339; 27.11. In the prose Amman Citadel Inscription (see K. P. Jackson, *The Ammonite Language of the Iron Age* [HSM 27; Chico, California: Scholars Press, 1983] 23 only "the gods" is possible. *B^e^nê 'ělōhîm* also occurs in Gen 6:2,4; Job 1:6; 2:1; 38:7 and *b^e^nê 'ēlîm* in Ps 29:1; 89:7. By either translation the expression is parallel to *b^e^nê 'ādām* in the prior colon. The scribe responsible for the alteration of the MT probably justified himself on the grounds that the the number of peoples, gods/angels and sons of Jacob was the same—seventy; see R. Tournay, "Les psaumes complexes (suite)," *RB* 56 (1949) 53.

35 So G; MT has transferred *Yiśrā'ēl* to v 9. As a result, *Ya'ăqōb* was moved down a verse and *'ammô* inserted. The G presupposes both the correct text and the MT, since it represents a conflation.

36 The text is dubious, but if there is a noun *yālēl*, perhaps we have a case of construct modifying absolute; cf. *pere' 'ādām* (Gen 16:12), *p^e^rîṣ ḥayyôt* (Isa 35:9), *'ōz melek* (Ps 99:4), *k^e^sîl 'ādām* (Prov 15:20).

37 For this translation see G. R. Driver, "Once Again: Birds in the Bible," *PEQ* 90 (1958) 56-57.

38 The sense of *yā'îr* is uncertain. G's *skepasai*, "covers, shelters, guards" makes sense but may be a guess. I assume a root *'wr* which yields *'ōrēr*, "rouse" and *'iwwēr*, "blind," Aramaic *'îr*, "awake," and post-biblical Hebrew *'ēr*. For a potential Ugaritic cognate, see Ginsberg, "Two North-Canaanite Letters from Ugarit," *BASOR* 72 (1958) 19 n. 11. On the translation "stir

up," see Driver, "Birds," or S. Loewenstamm, "Ugaritic Formulas of Greeting," *BASOR* 194 (1969) 54.

[39]In Ugaritic, *rḥp* seems to mean "swoop, stoop" (*CTA* 18.4.20,21,31,32; 19.1.31) but in *Ug5* 2.1.8 "fly" is more apt, or perhaps "hover" as here and in Gen 1:2.

[40]See Moran, "Song of Moses," 323-327.

[41]For a survey of similar expressions, see J. L. Crenshaw, "Wědōrēk 'al-bāmŏtê 'āreṣ," *CBQ* 34 (1972) 39-53.

[42]The G's "he fed him" is less likely, since it is a slightly easier reading and may be due to the influence of *wayyō(')kal* in the G *Vorlage* of v 15.

[43]On the paronomasia in this verse among words for "field," "mountain" and "breast," see my "On Hebrew *Śāde(h)*, 'Highland'" forthcoming in *VT*.

[44]On the much controverted word *d^e^bāš*, see A. Caquot, "*D^e^bāš*," *TWAT* 2 (1974) 135-139.

[45]Or "goats."

[46]Read with prior line for balance.

[47]Bashan was famed for its cattle—cf. Amos 4:1; Ezek 39:18; Ps 22:13.

[48]Literally, "kidney fat." Cf. "fat of wheat" in Ps 81:17; 147:14. "Fat" parallels "blood" of the next line.

[49]Cf. Gen 49:11 and Ugaritic *dm zt*, "olive oil," in *Ug5* 1.2.6 and *dm 'ṣm*, "trees' blood," i.e. "wine," in *CTA* 4.3.44, 4.38,59, 6.59; 17.6.6.

[50]One wonders whether *ḥāmer* is a variant or a gloss; it seems out of place, although the expected gloss would be the more common *yayin*. A remote possibility is that it is a gloss on v 15—**hămōr*.

[51]See Cross, *Canaanite Myth*, 50-52.

[52]Cf. Exod 3:17; 13:5; 33:3; Lev 20:24; Num 13:27; 14:8; 16:13,14; Deut 6:3; 11:9; 26:9,15; 27:3; 31:20; Josh 5:6; Jer 11:5; 32:22; Ezek 20:6,15.

[53]For a variety of examples see H. Gross, *Die Idee des ewigen und allgemeinen Weltfriedens in alten Orient und im Alten Testament* (Trierer theologische Studien 7; Trier: Paulinus, 1956) 70-83; Gaster, *Thespis*, 222; Patch, *Other World, passim.*

[54]*CTA* 3.2.39-41, 4.87-88.

[55]Gen 27:28; cf. v 39.

[56]*CTA* 6.3.6-7, 12-3.

[57]See H. W. Wolff, *Joel and Amos* (German original 1969; Hermeneia; Philadelphia, Pennsylvania: Fortress, 1977) 352-353.

[58]Wolff (*Joel and Amos*, 354) compares the perpetually fruitful trees of Ezek 47:12.

[59]Reading with G **wayyō(')kal Ya'ăqōb wayyiśba'*, presumably lost through homoioarchton; cf. Neh 9:25.

60 *Pace* Albright ("Some Remarks," 342), it is better to see in *ś^{e}ʿārûm* a unique cognate to Arabic *šaʿara*, "know," than to rewrite the verse.

61 The metaphor of father as mountain (quarry) is also attested in Isa 51:1; see N. A. van Uchelen, "Abraham als Felsen (Jes 51 1)," *ZAW* 80 (1968) 183-190.

62 The work was written after an Ephraimite defeat in a period of relative Judean security. Weiser (*Psalmen*, 368) thinks it is a reflection upon the battle of Gilboa (1 Samuel 31), yet, since we expect a work of the Davidic period to have a more conciliatory tone, it probably stems from the divided monarchy. Possible occasions are the defeat of Israel by Judah described in 2 Chronicles 13 or the depredations of Ben Hadad upon Baasha's Israel (1 Kgs 15:20) or of Hazael upon Jehu's (2 Kgs 10:32-33; Amos 1:3). Also possible is the subjugation of Israel by Tiglath-pileser III (2 Kgs 15:19). A Hezekian date, however, is favored because the phrase *q^{e}dôš Yiśrāʾēl* (v 41) is typical of Isaiah (2 Kgs 19:22; Isa 1:4; 5:19,24; 10:20; 12:6; 17:7; 29:19; 30:11,12,15; 31:1; 37:23). Though Ps 78:9 does not sound like a description of the fall of Samaria in 722/1, it might refer to a set-back that led to the three year siege, or perhaps to a failed sortie; see Clifford, "In Zion and David a New Beginning: An Interpretation of Psalm 78," *Traditions in Transformation* (Fs. F. M. Cross; eds. B. Halpern and J. D. Levenson; Winona Lake, Indiana: Eisenbrauns, 1981) 121-141; B. Halpern, *The Emergence of Israel in Canaan* (SBL Monographs 29; Chico, California: Scholars Press, 1983) 33-35, 41; J. Hofbauer, "Psalm 77/78, ein 'politisch Lied'," *ZKT* 89 (1967) 41-50; H. Junker, "Die Entstehungszeit des Ps. 78 und des Deuteronomiums," *Bib* 34 (1953) 487-500; Kirkpatrick, *Psalms* 2, 463; Kissane, *Psalms* 2, 32 and Dahood, *Psalms* 2 (AB 17, 1968), 238. A tenth century date is defended by A. F. Campbell ("Psalm 78: A Contribution to the Theology of Tenth Century Israel," *CBQ* 41 [1979] 51-79) and Eissfeldt (*Das Lied Moses*, 26-41). An exilic or post-exilic date for the received text of the psalm is advocated by H. A. Ewald (*Commentary on the Psalms* 2 [2 vols.; Theological Translation Fund Library 24; London/Edinburgh: Williams and Norgate, 1881] 255), Gunkel (*Psalmen*, 342), W. Barnes (*The Psalms* 2 [2 vols.; Westminster Commentaries; London: Methuen, 1931] 373), Briggs and Briggs (*Psalms* 2, 181) and R. Kittel (*Psalmen*, 289).

63 Since the right hand of Yahweh is never alluded to in contexts of creation, but only in contexts of battle (Exod 15:6 [*bis*],12; Ps 20:7; 21:9; 44:4; 60:7; 89:14; 98:1; 108:7; 118:15-16; 138:7), "acquired" is preferable to "created." Admittedly, *qānâ* =

"acquired by conquest" is unparalleled, but Exod 15:16; Isa 11:11 and Ps 74:2 refer to the acquisition or redemption of Israel from the enemy by *qānâ*. On the equivalence of the mountain and the land, see Moran, "Some Remarks," 327 n. 2 and add Isa 11:9; 57:13.

[64]The plagues serve as a transition, since they are in the memories of both the Exodus and Conquest generations.

[65]Vv 60-64 seem to refer to the battle of Ebenezer (1 Samuel 4). On the abandonment of the shrine of Shiloh, see Jer 7:12,14; 26:6,9 and the brief reports of I. Finkelstein, Ts. Lederman, Sh. Bonimovitch, "Shiloh, 1981," *IEJ* 32 (1982) 148-150; "Shiloh, 1983," *IEJ* 33 (1983) 267-268.

[66]We will again encounter the phenomenon of Ephraim bearing the brunt of the sinful past of *all* Israel in Exodus 32.

[67]MT has *ṣûrîm*, "mountains," but in all other passages only one mountain yields water. Dahood (*Psalms* 2, 240) sees here an enclitic *mēm*, but since the G reads the singular, the masoretic plural probably is anticipatory of *nôzᵉlîm* and is possibly also a reference to Exod 17:1-7 and Num 20:1-13, viewed as separate events. In either case, it is most likely inauthentic.

[68]G "them" is explanatory.

[69]Hebrew MSS are divided between *bᵉ*- and *kᵉ*-. G *hōs en* apparently is a conflation of both. For maximum variance, I read *bᵉ*- here (vs. *kᵉ*- in v 16).

[70]G singular; MT plural. For *tᵉhōm rabbâ*, cf. Amos 7:4; Ps 36:7; Isa 51:10. *Tᵉhōm* is also used of springs in Deut 8:7. See p. 48, n. 84. MT *tᵉhōmôt* anticipates *nᵉhārôt*.

[71]Though vocalized as a Hiphil with *hē'*-syncope (see GKC 53q), *lamrôt* could be re-vocalized **limrôt*.

[72]G reads **yiššātᵉpû*, which is possible.

[73]Cf. Exod 16:4,13; Josephus, *Antiquities* 3.1.6; the raining of honey in *CTA* 6.3.6,12 and the ironic allusions to a rain of food in Atra-Ḫasīs 3.1.34-35 and Gilgamesh 11.47-48.

[74]Noted by Kraus, *Psalmen* 1, 544.

[75]Vv 19-20 are an exilic addition from Dtr². On this passage see Friedman *Exile*, 23, and for the theory of two strata of Dtr see, besides Friedman, Cross, *Canaanite Myth*, 274-289 and R. D. Nelson, *The Double Redaction of the Deuteronomic History* (Sheffield: JSOT, 1981).

[76]G plural.

[77]G adds "your god."

[78]G omits "for forty years."

[79]G does not reflect *lō(')-yādaʿtā*.

[80]G plural.

81 G plural.

82 G *Vorlage* and Samaritan have *'ereṣ ṭôbâ* ***ûr(*^{e}*)ḥābâ* (cf. Exod 3:8), which could well be correct, the second adjective having been dropped by homoioteleuton.

83 G *hou* seems to reflect a confusion of *'ereṣ* and * *'ăšer.*

84 I follow the G in reading **w*^{e}*'ênōt t*^{e}*hōmōt*, parallel to *naḥălê mayim.* The MT's use to *t*^{e}*hōm* to denote an individual spring is disconcerting, while Gen 7:11; 8:2; Prov 8:28 afford analogies to the reconstruction.

85 G omits these conjunctions, perhaps reflecting a purer text.

86 G prefixes conjunction.

87 G adds "in them."

88 5QDeut (*Les 'petites grottes' de Qumrân* 1 [2 vols.; DJD 3; eds. M. Baillet, J. T. Milik, R. de Vaux; Oxford: Clarendon, 1962] 171) omits conjunction.

89 G adds "for you."

90 G "that."

91 Probably we should re-vocalize **n*^{e}*ḥaš.*

92 5QDeut reads *blbbkm*, but with *kāp sôpît.*

93 G prefixes conjunction.

94 G *ho kyrios.*

95 G has "I call to witness heaven and earth" as in 4:26; 5QDeut also has this reading, but as a gloss.

96 G "all his."

97 G singular, MT plural.

98 G, Samaritan, Theodotion "he."

99 G singular, MT plural.

100 G, Samaritan, Theodotion "he."

101 G plural, MT singular.

102 G singular, MT plural.

103 G reads *nātan* for MT *nōtēn.*

104 In the G all three begin "Hallelujah. Praise Yahweh," though the headings of Psalms 105 and 107 have been transferred in the MT to the ends of 104 and 106. Kirkpatrick (*Psalms* 3, 614), Kissane (*Psalms* 2, 159) and Briggs and Briggs (*Psalms* 2, 339-356) recognize the relationship between Psalms 105 and 106, while F. Delitzsch, mistakenly, in my opinion, believes that 104-107 form a unit (*Biblische Commentar über die Psalmen*^{3} [Leipzig: Dörffling und Franke, 1873] 185). For verbal contacts between the three psalms see the table on page 34.

105 References to exile and return in Ps 106:47 and 107:2-3 assure a post-exilic date for the group, while A. Hurvitz (*Bên lāšôn l*^{e}*lāšôn* [English title *The Transition Period in Biblical Hebrew*; Jerusalem: Bialik, 1972] 173) sees signs of late composition in Ps

106:30,43 and 107:3,30. Clifford ("Style and Purpose in Psalm 105," *Bib* 60 [1979] 427) notes parallels to Second Isaiah in emphasis on the patriarchs and Exodus. The psalmist must have the redacted Pentateuch, since he places the episode of the manna and quails (Exodus 16 [P]) before the gift of water (Exod 17:1-7; [E]). He also must antedate the Chronicler, since 1 Chr 16:8-22 quotes Ps 105:1-15.

[106] So G; MT has *šā'al* due to haplography with the following *wāw*.

[107] So MT; G reads **wayyābō(')*.

[108] G "rivers went" is due to the influence of the plural verb *hāl*^{e}*kû*.

[109] Literally, "lifted your hand."

[110] G translates *edōkan archēn*, "they appointed a leader." J. M. Myers (*Ezra-Nehemiah* [AB 14; Garden City, New York: Doubleday, 1965] 160) renders, on the other hand, "and determined to return." Myers seems to follow the opinion, attributed to P. Haupt and cited with approval by W. Rudolph (*Esra und Nehemia* [HAT 20; Tübingen: Mohr (Siebeck), 1949] 158), that *nātan rō(')š* is an idiom meaning "to set one's head in a direction." For a full discussion of the expression in this verse and in Num 14:4, see A. B. Ehrlich, *Randglossen zur hebräischen Bibel* 2 (7 vols.; Leipzig: Hinrich, 1909) 160. Ehrlich compares such phrases as *nātan qôl* or, especially, *nātan 'ōrep*; he might also have noted that, when *rō(')š* means "leader," it is always clearly stated of what the individual is a leader. We use a comparable expression in English when we speak of giving an animal or, by extension, a human, "its head." To take one's own head would be an act of rebellion; since the idiom in Hebrew only occurs in a context of strife, I have given it (perhaps improperly) a pejorative interpretation in my translation.

[111] MT has *b*^{e}*miryām*, "in their rebellion." Most likely the G is correct in reading **b*^{e}*miṣrayim* (cf. Num 14:4), and MT has lost a *ṣādê*.

[112] G does not reflect *s*^{e}*lîḥôt*. It may well be that **eleeōn* (cf. G Dan 9:9) dropped from the Greek due to its similarity to the following *eleemōn*.

[113] MT *wrb wḥsd* is simply an error—read *wrb *ḥsd*.

[114] G reads "these are your gods," apparently under the influence of Exod 32:4.

[115] G "us."

[116] G reflects **kol-'ēṣ ma'ăkāl lārôb*.

[117] G erroneously reads, instead of MT *wayyamrû* **wayyāmîrû*, "they exchanged"; we could, however, re-vocalize **wayyimrû*.

[118] For a full listing of the sources of Neh 9:6-37, see Myers, *Ezra, Nehemiah*, 167-169.

[119] I.e., he digs under mountains.

[120] Y^e*'ōrîm* elsewhere refers to channels of water, so here the poet speaks of underground rivers and the sources of springs. In the singular, of course, Y^e*'ōr* denotes the Nile (< Egyptian *'itrw*, "river").

[121] On the mythological and cosmological resonances of this verse see M. Pope, *Job*[3] (AB 15; Garden City, New York: Doubleday, 1973) 203.

[122] Whether or not chap. 28 is in its original setting, it is difficult to believe it is not from the same hand as the book of Job.

Chapter Three
MASSAH AND MERIBAH

In this chapter I increase the specificity further by analysing the legends of the waters that flow from a mountain or are associated with the names Massah and Meribah (Exod 17:1-7; Num 20:1-13). For comparative purposes, the traditions of Beer (Num 21:16-18) and Marah (Exod 15:23-26) are discussed first, even though they properly belong with the thirst stories of chapter one.

Beer

The simplest account of the miraculous production of water in the wilderness in the days of the desert wanderings of Israel is Num 21:16-18:

> *16*And thence [they traveled] to Beer [Well]; that is the well where Yahweh said to Moses: "Gather the people, and I will give them water."[1] *17*Then the children of Israel sang this song: "Rise, well,"[2] they sang[3] to it. *18*"O well which the princes dug, which the leaders of the people[4] hewed with scepter [and] staff."[5]

What can we make of this fragment? It is often described as archaic,[6] but such a dating largely reflects past scholarship's predisposition to regard short poems as the original form of Israelite tradition; the somewhat murky contents perhaps contribute to this evaluation. The lack of relative pronoun in 18a and of conjunction in 18c are insufficient grounds for assigning the poem an early date, especially since its present form seems garbled. In fact, the fragment is undatable, but its relation to the Massah-Meribah tradition is clear. Yahweh commands Moses to gather the people, and he himself will provide water. The editor[7] then quotes the opening of a song about a well that unspecified leaders of the people dug with their staffs; apparently he considers this miraculous. It seems, however, that the song has nothing to do with either Moses or Yahweh, but rather reports a fairly common event in the lives of the modern nomads and presumably also the ancient semi-nomads of Canaan. Western travellers have observed Bedouin elders locating underground sources and punching through the earth with their staffs, creating a well.[8] Our redactor, however, has chosen to associate the song with the miracle tradition whose fuller form is found in Exod 17:1-7 and Num 20:1-13. The "leaders" are analogous to Moses; the "walking sticks" correspond to his wonder-working rod.

Marah

The healing of the waters of Marah[9] is also related to the Massah-Meribah tradition. The source of Exod 15:23-26 is difficult to determine;[10] one could regard it simply as J's equivalent of Exod 17:2-7 (E), but the apparent familiarity of the northern Elijah-Elisha traditions with the tale suggests rather E.[11] The text itself presents few problems.

> *23*When they came to Marah, they could not drink the water[12] from Marah because it was bitter (that is why its name[13] is called Marah [Bitter]). *24*The people complained against Moses, saying, "What shall we drink?" *25*He[14] cried out to Yahweh, and Yahweh showed[15] him a stick,[16] and he threw it into the water, and the water became sweet. There he[17] established[18] for him[19] a statute[20] and an ordinance,[20] and there he tested him. *26*He said, "If you heed the voice of Yahweh your god and do what is right in his eyes and hearken to his commands and observe all his statutes, then I will not set upon you any of the illness that I made in Egypt,[21] for I, Yahweh, am your healer."

This story stresses Yahweh's ability to heal—he wards off (and inflicts) illness and makes salt water fresh. The same themes occur in Mesopotamia in the context of Creation ("Enki and Ninhursag")[22] and in Ezek 47:8-9 in the context of re-creation, but of this there is no hint here. Rather, the waters assuage thirst and symbolize Yahweh's healing power.[23] The testing of v 25 refers to the command of that verse, made explicit in v 26, rather than to a lost story of trial.[24] The command itself is a general bidding to heed Yahweh's word, a necessary preliminary to the more detailed covenant of Horeb. Exod 15:26 may be described as a covenant in miniature, inasmuch as it also describes the rewards of obedience. As at Beer, Yahweh provides drinking water through human employment of a stick, but that is the extent of the similarity.[25] New features that we will also see below in the Massah-Meribah accounts are thirst, complaint, lawgiving and testing.

Massah-Meribah

The incidents of Beer and Marah are never again mentioned in the Old Testament.[26] Massah and Meribah, on the other hand, are referred to repeatedly—Massah in Deut 6:16; 9:22; 33:8; Ps 95:8, Meribah in Num 20:24; 27:14; Deut 32:51; 33:8; Ezek 47:19; 48:28; Ps 81:8; 95:8; 106:32[27]. Since D uses only the name Massah and P only Meribah, many have tried to distinguish two separate traditions.[28] There hardly seems to be enough plot material to cover two stories, however, and to regard the parallel presence of both names in Exod 17:7; Deut 33:8 and Ps 95:4 as the result of glossation strains credulity.[29] These passages suggest, rather, that Massah and Meribah arose as poetic synonyms and that D favored *Massâ* because he wished to stress the testing of Yahweh (Deut 6:16), while P emphasized the rebellion of Moses and Aaron with the name *M^{e}rîbâ.*[30]

My investigation moves from poetic to prosaic texts, as is advisable where the double name indicates poetic antecedents. I will start with Deuteronomy 33, Psalm 81 and Psalm 95.[31] At first glance they seem to rely on a tradition largely unrelated to that of the pentateuchal narratives.

Deut 33:8-11

Deut 33:8-11 is difficult to date; the Blessing of Moses as a whole may go back to the eleventh or tenth century, but, except for v 11,[32] the blessing of Levi contains no orthographic, lexical or grammatical archaisms.[33] Vv 8-10 may therefore be a later insertion, but it is equally possible that scribal activity is responsible for the non-archaic features. Deuteronomy 33 seems to be of northern provenance, to judge from its exuberance in praise of Joseph (vv 13-17) and the emphasis on a *Levitic* priesthood employing Urim and Thummim in vv 8-11.[34] The text of vv 8-9 is rather corrupt, but with aid from the G and 4Q Testimonia the original form of the blessing is recoverable.

*8*And of Levi he said:
Give Levi your Thummim[35]
And your Urim to the man, your faithful one[36]
Whom you tried[37] at Massah,
Strove with[38] by the waters of Meribah,
*9*Who said to his father, "I do not recognize you,"[39]
And to his mother, "I do not know you."[40]
He did not acknowledge his brother[41]
And did not know his son.[42]
For they[43] obeyed your command,[44]
Kept your covenant.
*10*They teach your commandments to Jacob
And your Torah[45] to Israel.
They put incense in your nose
And a holocaust upon your altar.
*11*Bless, O Yahweh, his force;
Delight in the work of his hands.
Smite the hips[46] of his enemies.
Who of his foes can withstand him?[47]

We may infer that the tribe of Levi, here personified as Levi himself,[48] was granted the priesthood in the form of the Urim and Thummim as a reward for passing a test at Massah-Meribah. The ordeal was rejection of kin; by so doing they kept Yahweh's covenant. Wellhausen interprets this to refer to the Levites' (supposedly in this period a guild, not a tribe) renunciation of clan affiliation,[49] but the verb *t*^{e}*rîbēhû*, whether it means "strove against" or "strove for," indicates that a conflict took place. Moreover, even if "father," "mother" and "brother" denote the Levites' fellow Israelites, why are sons disowned? In fact, we know that consecrated individuals were not cut off from family.[50] It is more likely that the Levites renounce their kin in order to avoid the stigma associated with violence directed at a close relative.

The poem goes on to describe the function of the Levite. Notice how the ambiguity of the prefix conjugation is exploited in the last bicolon of v 9, for *yinṣōrû* refers both to the events of the past in the preceding lines and to the events of the present in the following. The blessing concludes in a martial vein appropriate to the role of the priest in holy war[51] and similar to the picture of the tribe of Levi in Genesis 34; 49:5-7 and Exod 32:26-29. V 11 thus fits the situation of strife presupposed in v 8.[52]

We can say somewhat more about this strife. The disavowal of *sons* in v 9 must be taken as a reference to fellow Levites. If there was internecine controversy, the rejected Levites are the objects of the verb *tᵉrîbēhû*, the faithful the objects of *nissîtô*. That Levi as a whole is blessed suggests that the bad Levites did not survive the strife.[53] That is, for cleansing itself, the tribe of Levi was granted the Urim and Thummim, whether this be a general reference to the priesthood or an allusion to a specific legend about the origin of the holy lots.

What do we learn of the events of Massah-Meribah from Deut 33:8-11? First, that there was water at Meribah (v 8). Moreover, that the tribe of Levi was tested there (v 8). There was a conflict in which Yahweh took part, striving both for and against the Levites (v 8). The Levites disavowed parents, siblings and offspring (v 9). Their action was connected with fidelity to the covenant (v 9).

Psalm 81

Psalm 81 is another text that alludes to the events at the waters of Meribah (the name Massah is not used). The reference to Joseph in v 6 is indicative of northern provenance;[54] Kraus's argument that "Joseph" simply denotes Israel in Egypt[55] is undermined by Ps 80:2, which refers to Joseph but not to the Exodus and is probably a product of the northern kingdom (v 3) antedating 722/1. It is a festival liturgy, perhaps of Sukkot,[56] with striking connections to prophecy.[57] I begin my translation after the superscription.

2 Sing to God, our strength;[58]
Shout to the god of Jacob.
3 Raise a song, play the drum,
The sweet harp with the lyre.
4 Blow the ram's horn on the New Moon
(And) on the Full Moon,[59] for our pilgrimage day.
5 For it is a statute of Israel,
A law of the god of Jacob;[60]
6 He established it as an ordinance in Joseph.[61]
When I[62] left the land of Egypt,[63]
I heard a language I did not know.[64]
7 I[65] removed his shoulder from[66] the load;
His lands left[67] the basket.
8 In distress you cried out, and I saved you;
I answered you from the covert of thunder.[68]
I tested [*bḥn*] you by the waters of Meribah (*selâ*).
9 Hear, my people, as I charge you;[69]
Israel, hear me!
10 There shall be no strange[70] god among you,
And you shall not bow down to a foreign[71] god.
11 I, Yahweh, am your god
Who brought you up from the land of Egypt.[72]
Open your mouth that I may fill it.[73]
12 But my people did not heed my voice;
Israel did not want me.
13 So I cast him[74] forth in the stubbornness of his heart;
They went according to their own counsels.[75]
14 If only my people would listen[76] to me,
If only Israel would walk in my ways.
15 Immediately[77] would I defeat their enemies;
Against their foes would I turn my hand.
16 The haters of Yahweh would cower before him,[78]
But their [Israel's] season[79] would be eternal.
17 I[80] would feed him from the choicest[81] of wheat
And sate him with honey from a mountain [*ṣûr*].[82]

What does this text tell us of Meribah? First, that it was an important event, since the psalm touches only highlights of the Exodus and Desert period. The reference to Meribah is directly preceded by an allusion to the Red Sea and followed by a *précis* of the covenant, for Ps 81:10-11 constitutes an inversion of Exod 20:2-3/Deut 5:6-7. Strikingly, the divine speech concludes with a promise of sustenance (v 11c) which is taken up in v 17. These verses echo the blessing of Deut 32:13-14, which were an exaggerated way of describing the mountain flowing with water, and hence constitute a reference to Meribah. As for the events that transpired, all we learn is that Israel was tested by Yahweh. This may contradict Deut 33:8, which says that some or all of the *Levites* were tested at Massah-Meribah, but echoes Exod 15:25-26; 16:4 in associating testing, law and sustenance. While Deut 33:8 suggests that some Levites passed their test and others failed, this passage implies that all the Israelites failed. The test of Meribah, according to Psalm 81, was to worship only Yahweh (v 9-10), the reward for which is food or drink (v 11). The people sinned, however, and were cast out (vv 12-13). Should they in the future repent, however, Yahweh will still reward them with victory and sustenance (vv 14-17). Psalm 81 is thus related to the passages examined in the previous chapter that link sustenance and apostasy. Those texts maintain that fertility leads to apostasy, while Psalm 81 says that, if only Israel were faithful, she would have ample food. The message is different, but the presence of the motifs of fertility, apostasy and Water in the Wilderness is not a coincidence. Psalm 81 also bears comparison with Exod 15:23-26 and Exod 16:4-5, inasmuch as testing, law and sustenance are associated. Note that, while the name Massah is not used, there is testing (*bḥn*)—another argument against divorcing the Massah and Meribah traditions.

Psalm 95

The final poetic text alluding to Massah and Meribah is Psalm 95.[83] It has much in common with Psalm 81. Both begin with calls to shout (*rnn, rwʿ*; Ps 81:2; 95:1-2) in praise of Yahweh, but they modulate quickly into a minor key (Ps 81:9; 95:7) by pleading with Israel to obey Yahweh. Both cite Meribah as a past example of disobedience (Ps 81:8; 95:8). While Psalm 81 ends with a forlorn promise of well-being, however, Psalm 95 concludes with Yahweh's punishment of the wilderness generation, though hope is expressed in v 7: "we would be his flock, if only you would hearken." Like Psalm 81, Psalm 95 has a cultic setting, and the psalmist speaks for Yahweh in the prophetic fashion. The divergence from pentateuchal narratives of Massah-Meribah in these psalms indicates a pre-exilic date, but whether Psalm 95 is northern or southern is difficult to say.

1 Come, let us sing to Yahweh;
Let us shout to the mountain of our victory.
2 Let us greet him with thanksgiving;
With songs let us shout to him.
3 For Yahweh is a great god
And the great king of all the gods,
4 In whose[84] hand are the depths[85] of the earth,
And the mountains' peaks[86] are his;
5 Who[87] owns the sea, which he made,
And the dry land which his hands molded.
6 Come, let us prostrate ourselves and bow;
Let us kneel[88] before Yahweh our maker.
7 For he would be our god and we his people,
His herd and the flock of his pasture[89]
Right now[90]—if only you would heed his voice.
8 Do not harden your heart as at Meribah,
As on the day of trial (*massâ*)[91] in the desert,
9 Where[92] your fathers tested me (*nissûnî*),
Tried me[93] (*b^{e}ḥānûnî*), although they had seen my deeds.[94]
10 For forty years I hated[95] that[96] generation,
And I said, "they[97] are a fickle[98] people,[99]
And they do not know my ways,"
11 Of whom I swore in my wrath
That they surely would not come to my abode.[100]

We learn from this psalm that at Meribah, on the day of trial, the Israelites were stubborn, doubting and testing Yahweh in some way, even though he had displayed his power. This differs from both Ps 81:8, where Yahweh tests the people, and Deut 33:8, where Yahweh tests Levi. Psalm 95 further implies that the forty years' wandering in the desert was decreed as the punishment for the sins of Meribah.[101] By synthesizing the evidence of Deut 33:8-9; Ps 81:8 and Ps 95:8-11 we may conclude 1)that the events of Massah-Meribah were of sufficient importance to warrant mention in these texts, 2)that there was water, 3)that there was an act of insubmission and covenant violation on the part of the Israelites, probably an act of apostasy (a feature of the Water in the Wilderness tradition in general), 4)that strife among the Levites took place, 5)that the Levites were consecrated to the service of Yahweh and 6)that Israel was punished with forty years of wandering in the desert. Any telling of the story should include most, though not necessarily all, of these elements. Testing or strife must occur to provide an etymological etiology, but our versions do not agree as to whether the strife and testing was of the Levites, Israel or Yahweh; this is yet another proof that etiological considerations do not necessarily motivate traditions, but that the reverse may be true.[102] In addition, since we have observed that the more general theme of Water in the Wilderness has connotations of fertility, we should be sensitive to such allusions in the Massah-Meribah tradition; we already have seen examples in Ps 81:11,17.

Exod 17:1-7

When we turn to the Priestly-Elohistic[103] account of Massah-Meribah (Exod 17:1-7), we find little that fits the poetic references.

> *1*All the community of the children of Israel journeyed
> from the desert of Sin on their travels, at the com-
> mand of Yahweh, and they camped at Rephidim, but
> there was no water for the people to drink. *2*The peo-
> ple strove (*wayyāreb*) with Moses, saying, "Give[104] us
> water that we may drink," but Moses said to them,
> "Why do you strive (*t^{e}rîbûn*) with me, and[105] why do
> you test (*t^{e}nassûn*) Yahweh?" *3*The people thirsted
> there for water, and the people complained[106] against
> Moses, saying, "Why did you take me[107] from Egypt
> to kill me and my children and my cattle[108] with
> thirst?" *4*So Moses cried to Yahweh, saying, "What
> can I do with this people; in a little while they will
> stone me!"[109] *5*Yahweh said to Moses, "Go before
> the[110] people and take with you some of the elders of
> Israel[111], and your rod,[112] with which you struck the
> Nile,[113] go and take in your hand. *6*I will be stand-
> ing before you there, on the mountain [*ṣûr*] in Horeb.

> Strike the mountain, and water will come out of it, so that the[114] people may drink." So Moses did, in the sight of the elders[115] of Israel. [7]He called the name of the[116] place Massah (Testing) and Meribah (Strife), on account of the strife (*rîb*) of the children of Israel and because they tested (*nassōtām*) Yahweh, saying, "Is Yahweh in our midst or not?"

Here we have no apostasy, no fertility, no strife among the Levites, no priestly ordination, no punishment—in short, none of the expected features of the Water in the Wilderness or the Massah-Meribah traditions, apart from the water itself and the *ṣûr* whence it flows. There is strife and testing, but they are directed by the Israelites against Moses and Yahweh respectively;[117] though they commit no apostasy, they doubt the deity's presence among them. It is unclear how this doubt is resolved in Exod 17:2-7. The process of partially reconciling this prose account with the poetic allusions studied above will shed much light on the history of the Massah-Meribah tradition and on the compositional method of the Elohist.

The key to the problem proves to be Exod 17:6, "I will be standing before you there, on the mountain in Horeb." Horeb here sounds like the name of a region.[118] Exod 33:6, however, refers to "Mount Horeb," and 1 Kgs 19:8 to "the mountain of God, Horeb."[119] Throughout D and Dtr, Horeb is the site of the lawgiving,[120] which is supposed to be a mountain.[121] Since *har* can mean both mountain and mountain country, a certain amount of ambiguity is inevitable;[122] note that Sinai, often called Mount Sinai, is in P also the name of a desert.[123] There was, however, in the desert of Horeb a specific mountain, called *har hā'ĕlōhîm* or *har Ḥōrēb*, which was the abode of the deity. "The *ṣûr* in Horeb" in Exod 17:7 must denote this mountain or at least part of it (cf. Exod 33:21-22 [J?]). Admittedly, scholars have generally presumed, influenced by Exod 19:1 (P), that the Sinai-Horeb pericope begins in Exodus 19, but under this assumption both the reference to Horeb here and the mention of the Mountain of God in 18:5 (cf. v 12) are incomprehensible.[124] Only C. M. Carmichael has successfully explained the received text. He argues that we must not view Exod 17:1-7 and 8-16 as unrelated fragments;[125] rather, while the people camp at Rephidim,

Moses goes ahead to Horeb (hence *šām* in Exod 17:6), where Yahweh is stationed. While he and the other leaders are absent, however, Amalek attacks the thirsty Israelites (cf. Deut 25:18). Moses, Aaron and Hur ascend a mountain (*gib'â*), which is probably to be identified as Horeb.[126] In other words, the Horeb pericope begins in Exodus 17. Massah and Meribah are either the names of the springs of Horeb or perhaps the site of the murmuring.

Exodus 32: Water and the Levites

The springs of Horeb are also alluded to in Exod 32:20, in the story of the golden calf,[127] likewise Elohistic.[128] After Moses returned from the mountain, he took the calf, burned it, ground it fine "and he sprinkled (it) upon the water and watered the children of Israel." Deut 9:21 also may refer to this flow: "The 'sin' which you had made, the calf, I took and burned with fire and ground it very fine and cast its dust into the wadi/brook that descends from the mountain."[129] We cannot be sure, however, if the wadi is running or not. There is yet a further, striking contact with the Massah-Meribah tradition in Exod 32:26-29.

> *26* Moses stood in the entrance of the camp and said, "Whoever is for Yahweh, to me!" and all the children of Levi gathered to him. *27* He said to them, "Thus says Yahweh, the god of Israel, 'Let each man put his sword upon his thigh and[130] pass back and forth in the camp, from one entrance to the other, and kill, each of you, his brother, his friend and his comrade'." *28* So the children of Levi acted according to the word of Moses, and about three thousand of the people fell on that day. *29* Moses said,[131] "You have been consecrated[132] [as priests] today to Yahweh, indeed,[133] each through[134] his son and his brother,[135] in order to set[136] today a blessing upon you.

Here we have another version of the events alluded to in Deut 33:8-11. In Exod 32:27 the Levites are commanded to kill *'aḥ, rēa'* and *qārôb*. The reference is apparently to fellow Israelites who worshipped the calf. If "*all* the children of Levi gathered" to Moses (v 26), these Israelites should have been exclusively non-Levitic. What, then, is the meaning of the reference to sons and brothers in v 29? Conceivably it means, reading an imperative with the MT, that the Levites are to consecrate themselves, every man inaugurating his son and brother. The conclusion, "in order to set today a blessing on you(rselves)" conforms with this interpretation. The preposition b^e- before "son" and "brother," however, does not fit.

On the other hand, the more likely interpretations proffered above, that the Levites were consecrated by means of or at the price of (the blood of) their brothers and sons, contradict the impression given by Exodus 32:26 (*kol-b*^{e}*nê Lēwî*) that all the Levites proved faithful. Gressmann sees the problem and concludes, as we saw above in discussing the parallel in Deut 33:9, that originally the tradition told of internecine strife.[137] Certainly all the Levites are not innocent if Aaron is among their number. The crux cannot be resolved by supposing that the story is so archaic that "Levite" here refers to a profession, rather than a tribe, for were this the case, instead of *b*^{e}*nê Lēwî* we would have *(*b*^{e}*nê*) *hall*^{e}*wîyîm*. For E, Levi is a tribe.[138] Exodus 32 seems dimly to reflect, if this interpretation of v 29 is correct, a tradition of the extirpation of apostate Levites comparable to Deut 33:9, with the survivors becoming the priests of Yahweh. In Exodus 32, Aaron is set off against his fellow Levites, and the legitimate consecration of the Levites as priests of Yahweh is contrasted with Aaron's usurpation of this function in v 5. Note that Deut 9:20 records that Yahweh almost killed Aaron for his role in the affair.[139]

According to Exodus 32, the Levites were awarded the priesthood at Horeb. Deuteronomy agrees, though at first glance it seems that they are consecrated at Jotbathah (Deut 10:7), rather than Horeb. Such is not the case, however. Deut 9:8-10:10 recounts the events at Horeb, and in Deut 10:1-5 the scene is still the mountain, and the subject is the tablets and the ark. In vv 6-7 we have an itinerary and then in vv 8-9 the consecration of the Levites to be the ark-bearers and bestowers of Yahweh's blessing. In v 10 we are back at Horeb, and only in verse 11 is Moses commanded to break camp. The inevitable conclusion is that vv 6-7 are either an interpolation or a digression,[140] but that in any event the Levites are consecrated at Horeb, as in Exodus.[141] The motivation for the inclusion of vv 6-7 is difficult to see; perhaps the author or glossator wished to tell at this point of the doom of Aaron, who had sinned so heinously at Horeb (cf. Deut 9:20).

P also agrees that the priests (Exod 40:12-15; Leviticus 9) and Levites (Num 3:5-13), whom he distinguishes, were inaugurated at the desert mountain, called by him Sinai. It is therefore clear that Israel attributed the institution of priesthood to the time of the sojourn about the mountain of Yahweh.

As we have seen, Deut 33:8-11 locates the ordination of the Levites at Massah-Meribah. By the present analysis this is similar to the Elohistic association of the springs of Massah and Meribah with Horeb, where the Levites are consecrated. Deut 33:9 also agrees closely, though not precisely, with Exodus 32 as to the act for which the Levites are rewarded with the priesthood. Like Phineas at Baal Peor (Num 25:6-13), they commit zealous mayhem, and most likely we should interpret Deut 33:11 in a similar fashion. In both Deut 33:8-9 and in Exodus 32 it is a little unclear whom the Levites kill, whether brother Levites, lay Israelites or both, yet the equivalence of the accounts is unmistakable. Since the calf is dissolved in the springs of Horeb, it is no misstatement to say that the rebellion of the golden calf takes place by the waters of Massah-Meribah, where the Levites punish the apostates and earn the priesthood of Yahweh.

Massah-Meribah and Fertility

Our analysis of the Water in the Wilderness motif noted that the miraculous waters often represent the fertility of Canaan. It is true that neither Exodus 17 nor 32 refers to fertility; in the former, the emphasis is on guidance through the wilderness and miraculous sustenance with water, while in the latter the water serves only to dissolve the calf. The nature of historical prose narrative allows only veiled allusions to fertility.

Horeb is described as a mountain on which Yahweh appears and as a mountain running with water. To the Israelite, this would conjure up, on the one hand, the image of the divine abode, whether Eden, Zion or all Canaan,[142] derived from the

Canaanite descriptions of the home of 'Ilu, and, on the other hand, the storm theophany of Yahweh, stemming from the poetry of Ba'lu. As we have seen, poetic texts describe the unidentified mountain as producing honey, oil, milk, swamps, rivers, deeps. E identifies this mountain with Horeb.[143] By putting, however, the creation of water before the thunder theophany of chap. 19, he obscures the mythological overtones. E employs the battle with Amalek in the same fashion, by implication locating it at the divine mountain in accordance with another traditional theme of Israelite literature with Canaanite antecedents—the *Völkerkampf*.[144] Finally, he refers to the theme of the banquet at the mountain of the gods in both Exod 18:12 and 24:11.[145]

Massah-Meribah and Apostasy

Recall that we perceived a theme of apostasy in both the Water in the Wilderness motif and in Psalm 81. In Exod 17:2-7, while there is doubt of Yahweh's presence, there is no overt apostasy. Exodus 32, on the other hand, is one of the classic *topoi* of religious infidelity in the Bible. Can the worship of the golden calf be the apostasy associated with the legend of Massah-Meribah? In order to decide we must study more closely the significance of the calf and the pre-history of Exodus 32.

That the story of the golden calf is, in its present form, directed at the iconography established by Jeroboam I at Bethel and Dan is widely acknowledged.[146] 1 Kgs 12:26-33 reports that that king, in order to forestall a return to Judean domination, had fashioned two golden bulls, saying, "You must no longer go to Jerusalem; here are your gods, Israel, who took you up from Egypt" (v 28). Jeroboam then installed one in Bethel and the other in Dan. He also cultivated the high places, appointing non-Levitical priests. He celebrated a festival and sacrificed before *both* bulls; we must suppose either that this took place before one was sent to Dan, or that it was a custom to march south with Dan's bull for the pilgrimage festival. Jeroboam also established his new priests in Bethel.

It is very likely that in the North the calves were considered to be the pedestal or throne of Yahweh,[147] but it is equally clear that to the authors of Exodus 32, 1 Kgs 12:25-33, 2 Chr 13:8 and Hos 8:6 the the bulls themselves were foci for the presence of Yahweh. Moreover, the Yahwist's law against "molten gods," was probably directed against the calves of the north.[148] Such a misrepresentation of the calves' significance is similar to the erroneous identification of statues with gods themselves.[149]

In the polemical Exodus 32, at any rate, the calf is an idol; it is identified as an *'ĕlōhîm* in v 1, and sacrifices are offered to it (v 8). Yet the author considers it a receptacle for the presence of *Yahweh* (32:5). This differs slightly from the apostasy of the Water in the Wilderness motif and Psalm 81, since the sin is Yahwistic idolatry rather than worship of other gods; i.e., the second, rather than the first, commandment (Christian enumeration) is violated.

Can the golden calf story be traced back beyond the anti-Jeroboam movement? Some argue that, like the ark and the bronze snake, the bulls of Israel must have been associated by their devotees with the desert period,[150] and that there must have been a tradition ascribing their fabrication to Moses or Aaron. Therefore, the Elohist or his source may not have been working from whole cloth, but may have been revising a cult legend. But even if such a legend existed, was it created in Jeroboam's day, or was it told by the priesthood of pre-monarchic Bethel, which may have been Aaronid (Judg 20:26-28)? Did Aaronid priests serve before the bull after the division of the kingdom?[151] The magnitude of the uncertainties warrants no speculation as to the antiquity of the tradition.

We may not conclude, then, that the Massah-Meribah tradition known to the non-pentateuchal authors was a polemic against the cult of the golden calf. Certainly E and D distinguish murmuring of Exod 17:2-7; Deut 6:16; 9:22 from the apostasy of Exodus 32; Deut 9:8-21, and we obtain no meaningful story by simply combining Exod 17:1-7 and Exodus 32. How, then, can we explain the contacts between these accounts?

Massah-Meribah and the Horeb Pericope

A full study of the Elohistic Horeb pericope[152] is beyond the scope of this work. It should be noted at the outset that it is composite; i.e., the Elohist used multiple sources, for chaps. 21-23 obviously had an independent existence, and chap. 24 contains separate strands.[153]

In creating a story of apostasy at Horeb, E drew upon older patterns of narration as well as individual traditions, including that of Massah-Meribah. As we have seen, the traditions had associations with water, testing, strife, apostasy, Levitical warfare and ordination, and punishent with death in the desert. Since we presume a main feature of the story was the Water in the Wilderness motif, Massah-Meribah contained an implied conditional promise of fertility, as well. Each of these elements finds its place in the Elohistic Horeb pericope, which begins in Exod 17:2. Exod 17:2-7 includes the etiological elements of strife and testing and the production of water, though the story is cast into the "murmuring" form.[154] One wonders whether Moses' hitting the mountain was part of the pre-Elohistic account; our poetic sources mention only Yahweh, Israel and the Levites. The remaining elements of the Massah-Meribah tradition appear at the end of the Horeb pericope—we have apostasy, punishment, Levitical strife and ordination.[155] The Elohist uses the Massah-Meribah tradition as an *inclusio* for his Horeb materials in two ways. First, the water of Horeb, symbol of fertility, reappears towards the end (in Exod 32:20), but more important, the unanswered question as to Yahweh's presence in the midst of the people (Exod 17:7) returns as the central topic of both chap. 32 and 33:1-11. Ironically, the answer proves to be "no." Israel tries to bring Yahweh near in the form of an idol, and for this sin Yahweh refuses to travel with the people at all (33:1-3), then relents slightly and agrees to travel with them *outside* the camp in a tent (33:7-11).

D and P display acquaintance with E's retelling of the Massah-Meribah story. While the former only alludes briefly to the tale (Deut 6:16; 8:15; 9:22), the latter gives us yet another version.

Meribath-Kadesh

P's version of Massah-Meribah is found in Num 20:1-13.[156] It seems to contain little independent tradition, but rather to be a polemical re-writing of various JE materials repugnant to the Zadokite priesthood.[157]

> *1*The children of Israel, all the community, came to the desert of Zin in the first month, and the people settled in Kadesh. There Miriam died and was buried. *2*But there was no water for the community, and they gathered against Moses and Aaron. *3*The people strove with Moses and said: "Would that we had perished when our brothers perished before Yahweh. *4*Why did you bring the congregation of Yahweh into this desert to die in it, us[158] and our cattle? *5*And why did you take us out of Egypt to bring us to this evil place, which is not a place of seed[159] or fig or vine or pomegranate, where there is no water to drink?" *6*Moses and Aaron went from before the congregation to the opening of the Tent of Assembly and fell on their faces. The Glory of Yahweh appeared to them *7*and Yahweh spoke to Moses as follows: *8*"Take the rod and gather the community, you and Aaron your brother, and speak to the crag [*sela'*] before their eyes, and it will give its water, and you[160] will produce for them water from the crag and you[160] will water the community and their cattle." *9*So Moses took the rod from before Yahweh as he[161] had commanded him, *10*and Moses and Aaron assembled the congregation before the face of the crag, and he said to them, "Listen,[162] you rebels! From this crag are we to produce water for you?" *11*Moses lifted his hand and struck the crag with the[163] rod twice ["two strokes"] and abundant water came forth, and the community and its cattle drank. *12*Yahweh said to Moses and Aaron, "Because you did not trust me[164] and sanctify me in the eyes of the children of Israel, you shall not bring this congregation into the land which I have given them." *13*Those are the waters of Meribah, where the children of Israel strove with Yahweh and he was sanctified among them.[165]

We note that the alternative word for the source of the water, *sela'*, is employed. That P himself was aware of the motif of fertility is shown by v 5, which emphasizes the sterility of the desert,[166] and perhaps by v 11, where the flow is characterized as *mayim rabbîm.*[167] Notice that P associates Meribah with Kadesh,[168] a fact given unwarranted significance by scholars who view much of the material dealing with Horeb, Sinai and Rephidim as originally pertaining to Kadesh.[169] P's intent in associating Meribah and the spy story with Kadesh is probably to harmonize the tradition reflected in Psalm 95 that Israel was punished with forty years in the desert at Meribah with both J's spy story, where Israel is similarly punished (Num 14:22-23), and Deut 1:19-46, where Moses' sin, the forty years and the spies are associated with Kadesh Barnea. Remember that in Deut 33:8-11 Yahweh was said to have tested some Levites and found them wanting; the motif of Levitic strife at Meribah appears in Moses' responsibility for the innocent Aaron's death and in the story's links to the Korah episode. An additional factor in the transferral to Kadesh was its association with Miriam's death; P treats, in a sense, the deaths of the three siblings in one section.[170]

Summary

This chapter has carried forward our investigation of the Water in the Wilderness motif of Chapter Two. There we discovered an intimate connection between the gift of water (and food) in the desert and apostasy. In Chapter Three we have seen that the traditions of Massah-Meribah conform to this pattern and include narrative elements shared with other accounts.

We first analysed Num 21:16-18, purportedly a record of Israel's leaders using rods to provide drinking water, whatever the song's original *Sitz im Leben.* Similarities to E's Massah-Meribah account were noted. We then turned to Exod 15:23-26, which features Moses, a stick or a tree, water, a commandment and testing; here, too, are elements of the Massah-Meribah tradition. Next we examined poetic references to Massah-Meribah in Deut 33:8-11, Psalm 81 and Psalm 95. These associate Massah-Meribah with water, strife, testing, violence among the Levites, ordination of the Levites, violation of the covenant through apostasy, fertility, forty years in the desert. We saw how E distributes these motifs between Exod 17:2-7 and Exod 32 in order to fabricate a new tale of apostasy appropriate to his needs. The Elohistic treatment of Massah-Meribah, locating it at the mountain of lawgiving, is strikingly reminiscent of Psalm 81 and also related to Exod 15:23-26.

The priestly retelling of the Meribah story arose out of a desire to harmonize conflicting traditions pertaining to the death of Moses and the forty years in the desert, as well as a need to account for the failure of Moses and Aaron to reach the promised land. Throughout, there is an attempt to load the guilt upon Moses and exonerate Aaron. The strife between Levites and Aaronids which is likely to have been part of the Massah-Meribah tradition is here transformed into a story in which Aaron is punished for Moses' wrongdoing.

Though references to apostasy and other forms of disobedience to Yahweh are abundant in the texts we have studied in this chapter, the fertility theme is veiled in the Elohistic and priestly materials. In Psalm 81, however, the water from the mountain is associated with honey and wheat. In P, a contrast is implied between the sterility of the desert and what ensues after Moses strikes the crag. In E, the location of the springs at the mountain of Yahweh reflects the Canaanite-Israelite image of the mountain of god as the center of fertility already familiar from the Zion tradition. Moreover, the parallelism between the covenant in the desert and the covenant in the land and between the apostasy in the desert and the apostasy in the land suggests that the irrigation in the desert parallels the fertilization of the land. The next chapter shows how the fertility theme comes to the fore in the literature of sixth and fifth centuries.

[1] G adds "to drink."

[2] G interprets the Hebrew consonants as ***‘ălê b^{e}’ēr*, "about the well," which is possible.

[3] Re-pointing ***‘ānû* to slightly improve sense. The MT's sequential imperatives with different subjects seem strange. Perhaps the G is right to read an imperative here but the preposition ***‘ălê* in the prior colon.

[4] G "peoples."

[5] Reading ***b^{e}miš‘enet*. MT has *b^{e}miš‘ănōtām*, "with their walking sticks," but more likely the final *mēm* of *b^{e}miš‘ănōtām* is a corruption due to the presence of the two *mēms* of the next word (Freedman, "Archaic Forms in Early Hebrew Poetry," *ZAW* 72 [1960] 106). The G is of no help, since the translator evidently forgot that *m^{e}ḥōqēq* may mean "staff" (cf. Gen 49:50) as well as "ruler" and went hopelessly astray. It is conceivable that the song continues "a gift from the desert," (so G. B. Gray, *A Critical and Exegetical Commentary on Numbers* [ICC; Edinburgh: Clark, 1903] 290) but this creates more problems than it solves.

[6] E.g., by P. J. Budd (*Numbers* [Word Bible Commentary 5; Waco, Texas: Word, 1984] 238), N. H. Snaith (*Leviticus and Numbers* [Century Bible; London: Nelson, 1967] 282) and Freedman ("Archaic Forms," 105-106).

[7] Perhaps J, to judge from the similarity of v 17a with Exod 15:1 (J; cf. the E doublet in Exod 15:20 [Cross, *Canaanite Myth*, 123]).

[8] J. Koenig, "Sourciers, thaumaturges et scribes," *RHR* 164 (1963) 20-25.

[9] The original pronunciation was **Marra*, as the biblical etymology and G transliteration *Merra* indicate. This invalidates E. Auerbach's (*Moses* [German original 1953; Detroit, Michigan: Wayne State, 1975] 71) derivation of the name from *mry*, "rebel," though paronomasia remains possible.

[10] On past scholarship see N. Lohfink, "'Ich bin Jahwe, dein Arzt' (Ex 15,26)," "*Ich will euer Gott werden*" (SBS 100; Stuttgart: Katholisches Bibelwerk, 1981) 29-41.

[11] The sequence of events in Exodus 15 is paralleled in 2 Kgs 2:12-22— the splitting of the water is followed by the healing of a spring. This corresponds to other parallelisms between Elijah, Elisha and Moses; see G. Fohrer, *Elia* (Abhandlungen zur Theologie des Alten und Neuen Testaments 31; Zürich: Zwingli, 1957) 55-58; R. A. Carlson, "Élie à l'Horeb," *VT* 19 (1969) 431-439; R. P. Carroll,

"The Elijah-Elisha Sagas: Some Remarks on Prophetic Succession in Ancient Israel," *VT* 19 (1969) 408-414.

Another sign of E is the presence of D-like phraseology in vv 25b-26; see Wright, "Deuteronomy, Introduction" (*IB* 2, 320); C. Brekelmans, "Die sogenannten deuteronomischen Elemente in Genesis bis Numeri. Ein Beitrag des Vorgeschichte des Deuteronomiums," *Volume du congrès, Genève, 1965* (VTSup 15; Leiden: Brill, 1966) 90-96. Note E's use of *nissâ* in Gen 22:1; Exod 20:20; 17:2,7, as opposed to J's sole use in Num 14:22. See below, p. 72-73, n. 24.

[12]G omits **mayim*, apparently through homoioarchton.

[13]G "the name of that place" is expansionistic.

[14]G "Moses" is expansionistic.

[15]G *edeixen*. *BHS* feels that his reflects **wayyar'ēhû* (cf. Samaritan) but the Greek regularly translates *hôrâ* with *deiknumi*; cf. Micha 4:2; Job 34:32 and the equivalence of *deiknumi* and *limmēd* in Deut 4:5; Isa 40:14.

[16]Or "a tree."

[17]"He" is probably Yahweh, though Moses (Auerbach, *Moses*, 71) cannot be excluded.

[18]G passive.

[19]Israel.

[20]G plural.

[21]G reads **miṣrîm*, "Egyptians." On the notorious diseases of the Egyptians, cf. Deut 7:15; 28:28,60 and the plague tradition (Exod 9:1-12; 11:5).

[22]In this myth, the sweetening of the waters is an etiology for the presence of the fresh water spring in the middle of the ocean that has given Dilmun its modern name *Baḥrayn*, "two seas."

[23]On Yahweh as healer see J. Hempel, "'Ich bin der Herr, dein Arzt,' (Ex. 15,26)" *TLZ* 82 (1957) 809-826.

[24]Many commentators regard vv 25b-26 as D (e.g., Noth, *Das zweite Buch Mose. Exodus* [ATD 5; Göttingen: Vandenhoeck & Ruprecht, 1968] 101), but in D the phrase is always in the plural—*ḥuqqîm ûmišpāṭîm*—(see Lohfink, "Ich bin Jahwe," 20, n. 22). Rather, we probably have E. Whenever Yahweh tests humans in E, he does so by delivering a command in order to see whether it will be obeyed (Gen 22:1; Exod 15:25; 16:4; 20:20). The Deuteronom(ist)ic writers change the notion; Israel is tested by affliction (Deut 8:16; Judg 2:22) or temptation (Deut 13:4). The issue of testing is relevant to the relation between Exod 15:23-26 and Exodus 16. Without attempting to solve the complex literary-critical problems of the latter (on which see B. S. Childs, *The Book of Exodus* [OTL; Philadelphia, Pennsylvania:

Westminster, 1974] 274-280), I would note the apparent presence of a pre-priestly stratum in 16:4-5 which likewise says that Yahweh "will test Israel, to see if he will walk according to my instruction/law or not" in respect to the manna. This text is also likely to be Elohistic, since Num 11:6 (E) presupposes precisely such a brief introduction of the manna as we have here. Hence it seems that Yahweh is portrayed as gradually schooling the Israelites in obedience as a preparation to the establishment of the covenant.

[25] Not surprisingly, a Jewish exegetical tradition identifies this stick/tree with Moses' rod; see G. Biename', *Moïse et le don de l'eau dans la tradition juive ancienne: targum et midrash* (AnBib 98; Rome: PBI, 1984) 32, n. 82.

[26] Ben Sira 38:5 refers to the story of Marah and Judg 9:21 to a place called Beer which may be the same as that of Num 21:16-18.

[27] To be more precise, the name Meribah occurs in the following forms: *M^{e}rîbâ* (Exod 17:7; Ps 95:8), *mê M^{e}rîbâ* (Num 20:13,24; Deut 33:8; Ps 81:8; 106:32), *mê M^{e}rîbat Qādēš* (Num 27:14; Deut 32:51; Ezekiel 48:28 [MT] and *mê M^{e}rîbôt Qādēš* (Ezek 47:19; 48:28 [G]). Many follow Dillmann (*Numeri, Deuteronomium und Josua*[5] [Kurzgefasstes exegetisches Handbuch zum Alten Testament; Leipzig: Hirzel, 1886] 417) in reading Deut 33:2 *mrbbt qdš* as **mmrbt qdš*. While this makes excellent sense, it would be the only example of the association of Meribah and Kadesh outside of P and Ezekiel, and in a text centuries older; Cross and Freedman (*Studies*, 97) date Deuteronomy 33 to the tenth century. Perhaps we should adopt Dillmann's alternative **mē'arbōt Qādēš*, "from the deserts of Kadesh," or follow Cross and Freedman (pp. 99,106) in reading **rib(^{e})bōt q^{e}dōšī[m]*, "myriads of holy ones."

[28] C. H. Cornill, "Beiträge zur Pentateuchkritik," *ZAW* 11 (1891) 20-34; Gressmann, *Mose*, 145-146, n. 1; Noth, *Exodus*, 111; S. Lehming, "Massa und Meriba," *ZAW* 73 (1961) 71-77; G. W. Coats, *Rebellion in the Wilderness* (Nashville: Abingdon, 1968) 53-71.

[29] Note, too, the association of testing with Meribah in Ps 81:8.

[30] If there was an actual spring, the name Meribah may have had a different origin entirely. In the ancient and modern Middle East, water rights are a subject of fierce contention; note the incidents of Gen 26:20-21, cited as parallels by H. Holzinger, *Exodus* (Kurzer Hand-commentar zum Alten Testament 2; Tübingen: Mohr [Siebeck], 1900) 60, and Exod 2:17.

[31] Psalm 106, clearly dependent upon Num 20:1-13, will be mentioned in the course of my discussion of the latter text.

[32] Cross and Freedman (*Yahwistic Poetry*, 113) conjecture that v 11 alone is the original blessing of Levi. In the opinion of C. J.

Labuschange ("The Tribes in the Blessing of Moses," *OTS* 19 [1974] 108-112), the blessing of Levi, vv 8-10, was inserted into the blessing of Judah, vv 7,11; see, too, Cassuto, "Deuteronomy Chapter XXXIII and the New Year in Ancient Israel" (1928), *Biblical and Oriental Studies* 1 (Jerusalem: Magnes, 1973) 58.

33See Cross and Freedman, *Yahwistic Poetry*, 97-122. *'Ăšer* (v 8), *'ēt* (v 9, *bis*) and the definite article (v 9) are all prosaic and atypical of archaic poetry.

34In the south the Aaronids preempted the priesthood, but in the north it was the prerogative of any Levite (Deuteronomy 18), and later even non-Levites (1 Kgs 12:31-32). On the history of the Levites, see A. H. J. Gunneweg, *Leviten und Priester* (Göttingen: Vandenhoeck & Ruprecht, 1965). The northern priesthood employs the Urim and Thummim in 1 Sam 14:41 (reading **tummîm*); 28:6. P later claims them, however, for the Aaronids (Exod 28:30; Lev 8:8; Num 27:21).

35MT reads *ûl(ᵉ)lēwî 'āmar tummêkā wᵉ'ûrêkā *lā'îš* [for MT *lᵉ'îš*] *ḥāsîdekā*, "and of Levi he said, 'Your Thummim and Urim to the man, your faithful one';" G has *kai tǭ Leui eipen dote Leui dēlous autou kai alētheian autou tǭ andrǭ tǭ hosiǭ*, "And to Levi he said, 'Give to Levi his [Yahweh's] Thummim and his Urim to the faithful man'." 4Q Testimonia (see J. M. Allegro, "Further Messianic References in Qumran Literature," *JBL* 75 [1956] 184 or Allegro, ed., *Qumran Cave 4 I (4Q158-4Q186)* [DJD 5; Oxford: Clarendon, 1968] 58) reads *llwy 'mr hbw llwy tmyk w'wrk l'yš ḥsydk*, "and of Levi he said, 'Give to Levi your Thummim and your Urim to the man, your faithful one'." Apparently G and 4Q Testimonia have the more original reading "give to Levi," lost by haplography in the MT with the preceding *ûl(ᵉ)lēwî*. Such a mistake should also have resulted in the loss of *'āmar*, so we must suppose the omission was in some period partially amended, perhaps by the careless scribe himself. A major problem remains, however, though it is not apparent in English. *Hābû* is the *plural* imperative, yet all the second person suffixes in vv 8-10 are *singular*. Hence, 4Q Testimonia is ungrammatical. In the G, the imperative is addressed to the people, and, due to the third person singular pronouns, there is no grammatical difficulty. G in the next bicolon has the verbs in the third person plural: *epeirasan, eloidorēsan*. There is unlikely to be an inadvertent textual error in either the Greek or the Hebrew but rather a conscious reinterpretation, whichever reading is original. It is *a priori* more likely that such a reinterpretation would occur in the process of translation rather than in the process of copying, i.e., that the Hebrew is original and the Greek secondary. Moreover, while the MT reading uniquely speaks of testing of and strife against Levi, the Greek reading conforms to other Biblical passages which describe strife against Moses and Aaron, both Levites. If the Hebrew *lectio difficilior* is more original, it is nevertheless ungrammatical and the product of error; the imperative must have been singular, either **hābâ* or **hab* (this form is unattested in the MT). I cannot imagine, however, why a scribe might have pluralized the verb. Perhaps it is due to manuscript damage rather than scribal carelessness. Note that the poet alludes to the formulaic request for an oracle—if so-and-so is true, *hābâ 'ûrîm*; and if so-and-so is true, *hābâ tummîm* (cf. 1 Sam 14:41, G). Loewenstamm (*"Haqd^{e}šat Lēwî la'ăbôdat h' b^{e}māsôrôt hattôrâ,"* *Eretz-Israel* 10 [1971] 169, n. 1) observes that only in Deut 33:8 does the order "Thummim...Urim" occur.

[36] The reading **ḥasdekā* is possible in place of MT *ḥasîdeka*, but it does not affect the interpretation.

[37] Eissfeldt ("Zwei verkannte militär-technische Termini im Alten Testament," *VT* 5 [1955] 235-238) implausibly sees here an allusion to military training.

[38] Or, depending upon the overall interpretation, "strove for" (Wellhausen, *Skizzen und Vorarbeiten* 2 [6 vols.; Berlin: Reimer, 1884-1899] 79, n. 2).

[39] Literally, "I do not see you."

[40] MT runs this line together with the line above, reading *hā'omēr l^{e}'ābîw ûl(^{e})'immô lō(') r^{e}'îtîw*; G *Vorlage* is identical save for the last word, which would have had the second person masculine plural suffix. 4Q Testimonia has *h'mr l'byw* ////// (erasure) *wl'mw lyd'tykhw* [*sic*]. Apparently, behind all these corruptions lies *hā'ōmēr l^{e}'ābîw lō(')* **r^{e}'îtîkā* (alternates *r^{e}'îtîhû/r^{e}'îtîw*) *ûl(^{e})'immô* **lō(')* **y^{e}da'tîk* (alternate **y^{e}da'tîhā*). The scribe of 4Q Testimonia seems to have at first written something like this, but later to have erased it in partial conformity to the proto-MT reading. Whether the second or third person suffixes are original is not possible to determine, though the former are more expected.

[41] MT "brothers." Either is possible.

[42] MT consonantal text singular; vocalization plural. Either is possible.

[43] G singular. Somewhere between vv 9 and 10 in the original text the number shifted, but it is impossible to know exactly where.

[44] G plural. To me it seems that *'imrâ* refers to the order to carry out the acts of v 9 and that the G reading erroneously anticipates the "laws" of v 10. 4Q Testimonia and Samaritan have the singular.

[45] Perhaps *twrtk* should be read **tôrōtekā*, "your laws."

[46] MT *mtnym* is a clear case of enclitic *mēm*. Read **motnê-m qāmāw* with Albright, "The Old Testament and Canaanite Language and Literature," *CBQ* 7 (1945) 22-23.

[47]M^e*śan'āw* is either a *casus pendens* "as for his enemies," or a misvocalization of **miśśōn*^{e}*'āw*, "of his enemies." *Min*, probably to be vocalized **man*, is either Ugaritic *mn*, Aramaic and Arabic *man*, Akkadian and Ethiopic *mannu*, "who," or else Ugaritic *mn(m)*, Akkadian *mannu(mme)*, "whoever" (Cross and Freedman [*Studies*, 113]). The verb is most likely to be read **y*^{e}*qîmennū* as in Gen 49:9; Num 24:9.

[48]Wellhausen (*Prolegomena*, 128-130), Meyer (*Israeliten*, 55-56), Gunneweg (*Leviten*, 43) and Cross (*Canaanite Myth*, 197) believe that "the man, your faithful one" is Moses (Baudissin [*apud* Gunneweg, *Priester*, 38, n. 2] suggests Aaron), but there is no evidence for this within Deuteronomy 33, especially since we now know that the phrase is parallel to Levi. Of course, these scholars are attempting a harmonization with Exod 17:1-7 and Num 20:1-13, but see my "The Rod of Aaron and the Sin of Moses," *JBL* (forthcoming) on the relation of the two. In any event, no passage describes Moses as renouncing his family.

[49]*Prolegomena*, 128-130; so also Meyer, *Israeliten*, 52. Whether or not the Levites were originally a tribe, their inclusion in the Blessing indicates that the compiler considered them as such; if vv 8-9 are a later addition, it is all the more unlikely that the process of becoming a Levite through renunciation of family is described (*pace* Wellhausen, Meyer, Gunneweg).

[50]J. Finkel ("Some Problems Relating to Ps. 95," *AJSLL* 50 [1933-4] 39-40) cites Hannah and Samuel (1 Samuel 1-2) and also compares to Deut 33:9 the testing of Abraham, who was ordered to kill his own son, in Genesis 22.

[51]Deut 20:2-4.

[52]H.-J. Zobel (*Stammesspruch und Geschichte* [BZAW 95; Berlin: Töpelmann, 1965] 31-32, 68) also sees in v 8 a reference to battles with competitors for the priesthood.

[53]Cf. Gressmann, *Mose*, 212, n. 1.

[54]See B.-Z. Luria, "*Mizmôrê t*^{e}*hillîm mē'eprayim*," *Beth Mikra* 23 (1978) 151-161. I do not agree with Luria, however, that Psalm 81 is a lament over the fall of Samaria. A more detailed and persuasive discussion is Loewenstamm, "*'Ēdût biyhôsēp*," *Eretz-Israel* 5 (1958) 80-82, which shows that the psalm is only distantly related to our pentateuchal materials and pertains to the living cultus of the north.

[55]H.-J. Kraus, *Psalmen* 2, 564.

[56]The issue is at which festivals the ram's horn (v 4) was sounded. According to the priestly code, the first day of the seventh month, the autumn new year, was a day of *t*^{e}*rû'â* (Lev 23:24; Num 29:1), P's term for a trumpet blast (cf. Lev 25:9; Num 10:5,6; 31:6).

Since the full moon of Tishri was a festival, Sukkot, one may conclude that our text was recited in the seventh month. Targum Jonathan in fact includes a notation to this effect, and other Rabbinic documents assume the same (see Loewenstamm, "*'Ēdût*," 81, nn. 10, 12). Unfortunately, the matter is not so simple. Note that horn calls are mandated for both new and full moon, yet we know of no full moon festival with this ritual. Num 10:10 (P), however, mandates *trumpet* calls on all festivals, including the New Moon. The preceding verses suggest that the shophar is simply part of the musical accompaniment; Gunkel (*Psalmen* 357) notes the use of horns in 2 Sam 6:15; Joel 2:1,15; Ps 150:3; 2 Chr 15:14. In short, we cannot ascertain the psalm's *Sitz im Leben* from biblical evidence and are left with Rabbinic testimony.

57 Loewenstamm ("*'Ēdût*," 81) notes that the cultic context (vv 2-5), the sudden switch to the divine first person (v 6) and the ensuing historical review (vv 6-13) and exhortation (v 14-17) suggest cult prophecy.

58 M. Dahood (*Psalms* 2, 263) reads **'ĕlōhê-m 'uzzēnû*, with enclitic *mēm*, in order to increase the parallelism with *'ĕlōhê Ya'ăqōb*. For a similar reason, one could read **'ĕlōhê mā'ôzēnû/mā'uzzēnû*, "the god of our refuge," as in Ps 43:2 (MT).

59 Here spelled *ksh*, rather than *ks'* as in Prov 7:20. The spelling with *'ālep* is more correct, cf. Ugaritic *ks'a* (*Ug5* 10.1.6), Punic *ks'* (*KAI* 43.13; note probable parallel with *ḥdš*) and Syriac *kes'a'*.

60 Or, reading **'hly* with Kissane (*Psalms* 2, 54), "a law of the tents of Jacob" (cf. Jer 30:18; Mal 2:12).

61 "Joseph" is here a people, not an individual. The name is only here spelled without the elision of the *hē'*; for other examples in biblical Hebrew, see GKC 53q. The form represents either a phonological archaism or a hypercorrection based upon the many names beginning either *yô-* or *yᵉhô-*, where this element is the divine name. Unlike other translators, I see this line as the end of a tricolon consisting of v 5-6a, since all three cola deal with lawgiving. At issue is whether the enigmatic v 6c is coordinate with v 6a or, as I believe, with v 6b.

62 Reading **bᵉṣē(')tî* to match *yāda'tî, 'ešma'*. On the similarity of *wāw* and *yôd*, especially in Herodian scripts, see Cross, "The Development of the Jewish Scripts," *The Bible and the Ancient Near East* (Fs. W. F. Albright; ed. G. E. Wright; Garden City, New York: Doubleday, 1961) 138-139, 176 and E. Qimron, "*Hahabḥānâ bên wāw lᵉyôd bit'ûdôt midbar Yᵉhûdâ*," *Beth Mikra* 18 (1972) 102-112.

63 On the use of *'al* with verbs of motion to mean "from" see Dahood, "Philological Notes on the Psalms," *TS* 14 (1953) 85-86. This

interpretation is supported by the G and is hence preferable to that of Loewenstamm ("*'Ēdût*," 81), who understands the verse to mean, "when he [Yahweh] went forth *against* the land of Egypt." Were Loewenstamm correct, however, I would still read *$*b^{e}$ṣē(')tî*.

64 Some (e.g. Gunkel, *Psalmen*, 357; Weiser, *Psalmen*, 377) see the cult prophet here referring to divine speech, but why should it be incomprehensible to him, and where else does a prophet burst out in this manner? Comparison with Ps 114:1 makes it more likely that v 6c goes together with v 6b in a bicolon. Apparently, Yahweh comments on the barbarism of the Egyptians' speech. G, however, reads the verbs in the third singular, referring to Israel, and this easier reading could well be original. If so, we should read b^{e}*ṣē(')tô* in v 6 with MT and G and suppose that the first person verbs of the MT are due to the influence of v 7.

65 G "he." Once again, either could be correct.

66 Dahood (*Psalms* 2, 265) regards this *mēm* as enclitic, which is possible but unnecessary.

67 G reflects **ta'ăbōdnâ*, "labored," but MT *ta'ăbōrnâ* makes better sense in parallel with v 8a—a simple case of *rêš-dālet* interchange.

68 The "covert of thunder" is the celestial storehouse of thunder and lightning, probably related to the "covert" and "tent" of 2 Sam 22(Ps 18):12. But is this a reference to Sinai or to the Red Sea? The former has clear associations with thunder (Exod 19:16; 20:18 [E]) yet the structure of the psalm suggests that the reference is to thundering over the sea. The storm theophany is associated with the Exodus in Ps 77:17-21, and the pillar of fire and cloud plays a role in Exod 14:19-20 (E),24 (J). A storm of some sort is also described in Exod 15:8,10. In addition, many texts refer to a battle between the storm god and the sea; see above, p. 41-42, n. 27. On the whole, it is likely that Ps 81:8a refers to Israel's cry of desperation at the sea and v 8b to Yahweh's response in thunder.

69 This verse has apparently suffered expansion in the G, perhaps through the influence of Ps 50:7, as it presupposes *$*š^{e}$ma' 'ammî wa'ădabbērâ*.

70 The adjective *zār* also describes foreign gods in Deut 32:16; Isa 43:12; Ps 44:21.

71 *Nēkār* is similarly used in Deut 32:12; Mal 2:11; Dan 11:39.

72 This verse has close parallels in Exod 20:2; 29:46; Lev 11:45; 19:36; 22:32-33; 25:38; 26:13; Num 15:41; Deut 5:6; Judg 6:8; 1 Sam 10:18; Amos 2:10. For a general discussion see W. Zimmerli, "Ich bin Jahwe," *Geschichte und Altes Testament* (Fs. A. Alt; Beiträge zur historischen Theologie 16; Tübingen: Mohr [Siebeck], 1953) 179-209.

73 Here, too, Gunkel (*Psalmen*, 357-358) sees a reference to prophecy,

but this is not the natural reading of the verse, especially in light of v 17.

[74] G has "them."

[75] *Š^{e}rîrût lēb* also occurs in Deut 29:18. Ps 81:13 as a whole is similar to recurring phraseology in the prose oracles of Jeremiah; cf. Jer 3:17; 7:24; 9:13; 11:8; 13:10; 16:12; 18:12; 23:17. Cf. also Micah 6:16.

[76] Restoring *'my [y]šm'*, the *yôd* having been dropped by haplography.

[77] G misunderstands *kim'aṭ* and translates, "I would reduce their enemies to nothing."

[78] Cf. similar phraseology in 2 Sam 22(Ps 18):45; Ps 66:3. On the possible translation of *kḥš* as "diminish" see J. H. Eaton, "Some Questions of Philology and Exegesis in the Psalms," *JTS* 19 (1968) 603-604.

[79] This translation is tentative; see Kissane, *Psalms* 2, 56. By "season" I mean "good season." Such a rendering is preferable to the usual "doom" or the like, since it smoothes the transition into v 17. Eaton ("Some Questions," 607-608) suggests "oppression" < **'ny*, "to be afflicted," but such an elision of the end of a III-y root is strange; *'ēt*, "occasion," is not a fair parallel, since it probably is the infinitive of the root *y'd*, "to meet."

[80] Though biblical Hebrew is quite capricious in this regard, we still expect to find the same person in the verbs of v 17. Accordingly, I assume a dittography of the *wāw*, which in the Herodian period was often identical to *yôd*, and read **wā'ōkîlēhû*. G has both verbs in the third person, however; we must consider these as ancient variants between which we cannot choose. The situation of the accusative pronominal suffixes is even more confused; G has third person masculine plural for both, while MT has third singular in 17a and second singular in 17b. Perhaps, then, the discordance of the verbs is not due to scribal error, but rather to the desire to incorporate as many variants as possible, both in respect to verb and to suffix.

[81] Literally, "fat" (cf. Deut 32:14; Ps 147:14). Oesterly (*Psalms* 2, 372) pertinently compares English "cream," meaning "best."

[82] An allusion to Deut 32:13.

[83] For a thorough survey of scholarship see G. H. Davies, "Psalm 95," *ZAW* 85 (1973) 183-195.

[84] *'Ăšer* is suspect, since it overloads the line (*BHS*).

[85] G *perata* is based upon **merḥaqqê*, as opposed to MT *meḥq^{e}rê*. G has the *lectio facilior*, since *'ereṣ merḥaq* is found in Isa 13:5; 46:11; Jer 4:16; 6:20; Prov 25:25; the parallel with *hārîm*, however, suggests that the MT "depths," the *lectio difficilior*, is original. Cf. the use of *ḥēqer* for the depths of the earth in Job 38:16.

86 No convincing etymology has been found for the word *tô'āpôt*, which appears in Num 23:22; 24:8; Ps 95:4; Job 22:25. The attempt of F. Rundgren ("Zum Lexicon des Alten Testaments," *ActOr* 21 [1953] 316-325) to derive the word, via Aramaic, from a root *ḏ'p*, "to be doubled," suffers from chronological problems, since he posits an Aramaic-like development **taḏ'apāt* (actually, Rundgren has "**taḏ'apōt!*) > **ta''apāt* > **ta''apāt* (by dissimilation), whereupon the Canaanite shifts *a'* > *ā* > *ō* transpired. The first process, however, occurred in the first millennium, while the latter shifts took place in the second. The most likely cognate still is Arabic *yafa'un*, "hill." Note that the poet puns with the ancient *tô'ǎpōt r^e'ēm* (Num 23:22; 24:8).

87 The relative pronoun is here, too, suspect (*BHS*).

88 G "let us weep" is based upon an erroneous **w^enibke(h)* for MT *w^enibr^ekâ*.

89 MT has "for he is our god and we the people of his herd and the flock of his pasture," but the cola are extremely unbalanced. Accordingly, I read **'ammô*. The similar passages Ps 79:13; 100:3 support this reading. On the other hand, divergence from these latter texts may indicate that once more the poet is modifying traditional phraseology. On the translation of *yād* as "pasture" see Finkel, "Some Problems," 37.

90 Literally, "this day."

91 *Massâ* is not a place name here, but the psalmist demonstrates his knowledge of a trial at Meribah by his use of the roots *nsh* and *bḥn*.

92 "Where" is the etymological translation of *'ǎšer*; "when," however, is equally possible. On the testing of Yahweh cf. Exod 17:2,7; Deut 6:16; Judg 6:39; Isa 7:12; Ps 78:18,41,56; 106:14. It means either to try Yahweh's patience (Ps 78:41,56) or to request a miracle from him to test his power (Judg 6:39; Isa 7:12; Ps 78:18; 106:14). We saw a corresponding polyvalence in the motif of the testing of Israel, which could mean either the affliction or temptation of Israel, or the issuing of commands (p. 72-73, n. 24).

93 G omits "me."

94 MT singular; G plural. Either is possible.

95 *Qwṭ* is generally supposed to be an allo-form of *qwṣ*, "to loathe" (BDB, KB). Finkel ("Some Problems," 32-34) translates *'āqûṭ* as "I shepherded" on the basis of Aramaic and Arabic *qwṭ*. The context, which is negative in tone, argues against this interpretation, as do the uses of this root in the Niphal in Ezek 6:9 (vocalized as though from **qṭṭ*); 20:43; 36:31; Job 10:1 (vocalized as though from **nqṭ*) and in the Hithpolel in Ps 119:158; 139:21, clearly meaning "to loathe."

[96]G has *tę̄ geneą ekeinę̄* presumably reading, as do I, **baddôr*, rather than the masoretic *b^e dôr*.

[97]G omits "they," probably lost by haplography with the following *hēm*. If, however, either *hēm* in the MT is dittographic, it is more likely to be the second.

[98]Literally, "of errant heart."

[99]G has *aei*, apparently reading **(mē)'ôlām* for MT *'am*. The received text is preferable.

[100]*M^e nûḥâ*, "(place of) rest."

[101]Below, p. 68, I will argue that P either interpreted Psalm 95 in this fashion or else knew another tradition that linked Meribah with the forty years in the desert. Compare the expulsion of the Israelites in Ps 81:13 in the aftermath of the sin of Meribah.

[102]On biblical etiologies, see B. O. Long, *The Problem of Etiological Narrative in the Old Testment* (BZAW 108; Berlin: Töpelmann, 1968).

[103]Exod 17:1 is a contribution of the priestly redactor; it has a close parallel in the way station list, Num 33:14. The name Rephidim is native to the Elohistic account of the battle with Amalek in Exod 17:8-16, and P correctly deduced that the story of Massah-Meribah transpired in the same locale, near the Sinai desert (Num 33:15).

Exod 17:2-7 is Elohistic. Many scholars have attributed the bulk of these verses to J, simply because this is conventional wherever there is doubt, but then they must suppose a massive process of textual conflation and glossation; cf., *inter alios*, Noth (*Exodus*, 109-112), Coats (*Rebellion*, 5). Older scholars such as Cornill ("Beiträge"), S. R. Driver (*The Book of Exodus* [Cambridge Bible for Schools and Colleges; Cambridge: University, 1911] 154-158) and A. H. McNeile (*The Book of Exodus*[2] [Westminster Commentaries; London: Methuen, 1917] 100-102) and a recent writer such as A. Jenks (*The Elohist and North Israelite Traditions* [SBL Monograph 22; Missoula, Montana: Scholars Press, 1977] 43) see a composite text that is basically E. For a more detailed survey of views see V. Fritz, *Israel in der Wüste* (Marburger theologische Studien 7; Marburg: Elwert, 1970) 11, n. 6. *Pace* Gressmann (*Mose*, 145-146, n. 1), two complete narratives cannot be derived from Exod 17:2-7; see Childs, *Exodus*, 306. The double name of the spring rather derives from poetic form. The alleged (by Koenig, "Sourciers," 30 and many others) redundancy of vv 2-3 is non-existent; there is instead a progression— Israel finds no water, the people complain, Moses dismisses them impatiently, displaying lack of trust in Yahweh (v 2); the people begin to thirst and actually wish they had never left Egypt, and

Moses finally turns to Yahweh (v 3). Similarly, the striving and testing are not redundant; the people strive with Moses but test Yahweh. We have a seamless text in vv 2-7, and all evidence indicates that it is Elohistic. Noth (*Überlieferungsgeschichtliche Studien* 1 [Schriften der Königsberger gelehrten Gesellschaft, geisteswissenschaftliches Klasse 18:2; The Halle: Niemeyer, 1943] 29) rejects the common view that Horeb here (or anywhere) is a sign of E (vs. Holzinger, *Einleitung in den Hexateuch* [Freiburg: Mohr (Siebeck), 1893] 182; S. R. Driver, *An Introduction to the Literature of the Old Testament*[2] [Edinburgh: Clark, 1891] 119; Eissfeldt, *Einleitung in das Alte Testament*[3] [Tübingen: Mohr (Siebeck), 1964] 243) and in fact deletes it wherever it occurs in the Tetrateuch (Exod 3:1; 17:6; 33:6). His view that "in Horeb" is here an addition is endorsed by a host of scholars, including Fritz (*Wüste*, 11), H. Seebass (*Mose und Aaron, Sinai und Gottesberg* [Abhandlungen zur evangelischen Theologie 2; Bonn: Bouvier, 1962] 5), L. Perlitt ("Sinai und Horeb," *Beiträge zur Alttestamentlichen Theologie* [Fs. W. Zimmerli; ed. H. Donner, R. Hanhart, R. Smend; Göttingen: Vandenhoeck & Ruprecht, 1977] 309), P. Weimar (*Die Berufung des Mose* [Orbis Biblicus et Orientalis 32; Göttingen: Vandenhoeck & Ruprecht, 1980] 339) and W. H. Schmidt (*Exodus, Sinai und Mose* [Ertrage der Forschung 191; Darmstadt: Wissenschaftliche Buchgesellschaft, 1983] 100); these scholars were anticipated by Gressmann (*Mose*, 146, n.) and Baentsch (*apud* Fritz, 11, n. 8). Yet why would a glossator locate Massah-Meribah at Horeb? Glosses are intended to lessen, not heighten, confusion. It is a fact that D only uses Horeb and P and J only Sinai to denote Yahweh's mountain, so it is reasonable that E should use only Horeb. Perhaps part of the problem is the aforesaid scholars' inability to make sense of *bᵉḥōrēb* in Exod 17:6; it can be explained, however (see below, p. 60ff.). Another indicator of E is the prominence of the rod (v 5), which makes frequent appearances in the hand of Moses in the Elohistic source (Exod 4:17; 7:17,20; 9:23; 10:13; the source of 4:2,4; 7:15; 14:16 is uncertain, though here, too, I favor attribution to E), sometimes under the title *maṭṭē(h) hāʾĕlōhîm* (Exod 4:20; 17:9). Finally, the elders appear only in E (Exod 3:18; 19:7; 24:1,9,14; Num 11:16,24,25,30).

104 The verb is plural in the MT (*tᵉnû*), but singular in the G, reflecting either **tēn* or **tᵉnâ* (cf. Num 11:13). As the *lectio difficilior*, the MT is probably correct, in which case the addressees are Moses and Yahweh. Moreover, the response of Moses presupposes that the request had been addressed to both himself and Yahweh, rather than to Moses and Aaron as Cassuto (*A Commentary on*

the Book of Exodus [Hebrew original 1951; Jerusalem: Magnes, 1967] 201) would have it.

105 MT lacks "and," which is in the Versions. That the prior word ends in *yôd* suggests that the G *Vorlage* is correct and that MT suffered a *yôd-wāw* haplography.

106 G adds "there," probably expansionistically. The inspiration is the "there" of the prior clause.

107 Reading, to fit the context, **heʿělîtānî* for *heʿělîtānû*.

108 G has "us...our children." Rather than reconstruct a variant consonantal text, it is easier to believe that pluralization occurred in the process of translation. MT and G agree in reading *bny* and *mqny* as plural, but both could be singular.

109 MT has *sᵉqālūnî*, with which G concurs. A reading **sᵉqālānî*, however, is also possible; in this story *ʿam* usually takes singular verbs, the other exception being *wayyō(ʾ)mᵉrû*.

110 G "this people" seems to be the result, either in the Hebrew *Vorlage* or in the process of transmission in Greek, of a vertical dittography from the previous verse.

111 G "elders of the people."

112 G "the rod." The semantics of the words *maṭṭe(h)* and *šēbeṭ* have not, to my knowledge, been adequately explored. BDB, 641 maintains that they mean both "rod" and "tribe" because the tribal leader carried a staff. The root of the *maṭṭe(h), nṭy*, however, means to stretch out; a staff may be stretched out, but it is more usually leaned upon. Perhaps the original meaning of *maṭṭe(h)* was "branch" (Ezek 19:11,12,14), which moved naturally into both "rod" and "tribe." *Šēbeṭ* could have followed suit by analogy. We need not think only of our notion of "family tree"; the ancient world is full of the metaphorical description of the family as "root," "stalk," "seed," "fruit" etc. The equivalent in English would be "stock" or in German "Stamm."

113 The source division of the plague narrative is notoriously treacherous. At least Exod 7:17 and probably v 20b reflect the Elohistic tradition that Yahweh himself, or his proxy Moses, used the rod of God (to be taken literally; see Loewenstamm, "*Maṭṭe(h),*" *ʾEnṣiqlôpedyâ Miqrāʾît* 4, 826-828) to smite the Nile.

114 Some G versions read "my."

115 G "children." Either these are ancient variants, between which we cannot chose, or else the full text was **lᵉʿênê ziqnê bᵉnê Yiśrāʾēl* (cf. Exod 4:29), which suffered different haplographies by homoioteleuton in both MT and G *Vorlage* (or in the process of the translation of the G).

116 G adds *ekeinou.*

117 Most likely they test Yahweh's power, rather than his patience, by

seeking a miracle (v 2) and proof of his presence (v 7).

118 So Clifford, *Mountain*, 121-122.

119 So MT; G has "Mount Horeb." If MT is original, *hā'ĕlōhîm* must have fallen out of the G *Vorlage* or been omitted in the act of translation due to the similarity of *hē'* and *ḥêt*. Exod 3:1 also in the MT reads "the mountain of God, Horeb," but the Hebrew locative suffix makes it unclear whether Horeb is the mountain or the region in which it is located; here, too, G does not read *hā'ĕlōhîm*.

I will not discuss the location of Horeb and Sinai. Perlitt ("Sinai und Horeb," 302-322) points out that the former seems to be in Midian and the latter in Edom. The name *Ḥōrēb* may most easily be explained as meaning "the angry one" (if < *ḥrb*; cf. Arabic *ḥaraba*) or "the destroyer" (if < *ḫrb*; cf. Rabbinic Hebrew *ḥārab* and Arabic *ḫaraba*), but Perlitt (pp. 315-318) translates "the desolate one," comparing the form *šōmēm*.

120 Deut 1:2,6,19; 4:10,15; 5:2; 9:8; 18:16; 28:69; 1 Kgs 8:9=2 Chr 5:10; also Mal 3:22; Ps 106:19.

121 Deut 5:4,19; 9:9,10; 10:1,3,4. Note that Deut 1:6 calls Horeb "this mountain."

122 See D. M. Beegle, *Moses, the Servant of Yahweh* (Grand Rapids, Michigan: Eerdmans, 1972) 185.

123 Exod 19:1,2; Lev 7:38; Num 1:1,19; 3:4,14; 9:1,5; 10:12; 26:64; 33:15,16. Cf. the desert of Sin (Exod 16:1; 17:1; Num 33:11,12). Seemingly, Sinai is also a region in the archaic texts Deut 33:2; Jud 5:5 and Ps 68:9. For details see Perlitt, "Sinai und Horeb," 303-305.

124 Hence the attempts to see *bᵉḥōrēb* as a gloss, and the common view that chap. 18 is "misplaced"; see Ibn Ezra, Driver (*Exodus*, 162), McNeile (*Exodus*, 106-107), Beegle (*Moses*, 192). Though an adherent of the supplement theory and reckoning *bᵉḥōrēb* as an addition, E. Zenger (*Israel am Sinai* [Altenberge: CIS, 1982] 74-75) at least tries to account for its addition, unconsciously following the Rabbinic approach (see Biename', *Moïse et le don de l'eau, passim*) of seeing the water of Horeb as a symbol of the covenant; moreover, he notes the connection with the fertility of Ezekiel 47 (cf. below, pp. 98-99). As for Exodus 18, while it is true that Deut 1:9-18 seems to locate the events of Exod 18:13-26 at a different time, my concern is with the events specific to Horeb, i.e., vv 1-12,27.

125 *The Laws of Deuteronomy* (Ithaca, New York: Cornell, 1974) 244-245. Carmichael does not discuss source attribution, but Exod 17:8-16 has all the earmarks of E—Joshua, Aaron, Hur, the rod of God—as was recognized by older scholars (e.g. Driver,

Introduction, 30). More recently, Noth (*Exodus*, 112-115) and J. H. Grønbaek ("Juda und Amalek: Überlieferungsgeschichtliche Erwägungen zu Exodus 17,18-16," *ST* 18 [1964] 26-45) attribute the text to J, and Eissfeldt ("Die älteste Erzählung vom Sinaibund," *ZAW* 73 [1961] 138-139) sees a separate source altogether. While it is true we would expect Judahite traditions about the Amalekites, who also lived in the south, this cannot be the sole criterion for source evaluation. It is particularly difficult to see the rod of God as an addition on the basis of an alleged contradiction between Moses' raising the rod and his raising his hand(s), because the rod is the *nēs* that motivates the name *Yahwe(h) nissî*; for the use of *nēs* to mean "pole," see Num 21:8-9. Note, moreover, the alternation between hand and rod in Exod 9:22-23; 10:12,13 and Isa 49:22.

[126]The identification of this *gib'â* with Horeb, first proposed by Ibn-Ezra (*ad loc.*), is suggested by the context and also by the erection of an altar. On the mythological background of this incident see below, pp. 89-90, n. 144.

[127]*'Ēgel* is more accurately translated "young bull," as McNeile (*Exodus*, 205) stresses.

[128]Most commentators regard Exodus 32 as composite, with the predominant source either E (W. Beyerlin, *Herkunft und Geschichte des ältesten Sinaitraditionen* [Tübingen: Mohr (Siebeck), 1961] 24-28, 144-153) or J (Noth, *Exodus*, 198-207; Coats, *Rebellion*, 186). Lehming, "Versuch zu Ex. XXXII," *VT* 10 [1960] 16-50] claims to discern *twelve* stages of tradition and text, including a good deal of Yahwistic material. W. Rudolph (*Der "Elohist" von Exodus bis Josua* [Berlin: Töpelmann, 1938] 48-53) and Childs (*Exodus*, 558-562), on the other hand, stress the unity of the chapter. Childs inclines towards J, with interpolation of vv 7-14 (D) and vv 25-29. I believe that Beyerlin makes a convincing case for the attribution to E and that Childs and Rudolph are correct in stressing the unity of the text, but do not go far enough. The entire story presupposes Exod 24:12-15a, 18b, the ascent of the mountain by Moses and Joshua, Aaron's appointment as leader (along with Hur) and a lengthy absence of forty days. The reference to Elohim in 24:13 and the contacts with Exod 17:8-16 show we are in E. Also, the location of the people at the foot of the mountain (Exod 32:19) echoes 19:16b-17. Finally, the story's continuation in 33:6 refers to Mount Horeb (cf. Ps 106:19). Beyerlin sees several levels of E, but no J or P.

Of all the internal contradictions supposed by various commentators, however, not one convinces. Aaron's fabrication of the calf in v 4 is not contradicted by v 24, where he claims that the calf emerged spontaneously from the fire; as most recognize, we have here a realistic portrayal of a culprit, caught red-handed, frantically trying to exonerate himself (Gressmann, *Mose*, 202; Driver, *Exodus*, 353-354; McNeile, *Exodus*, 207; Noth, *Exodus*, 201; M. Aberbach, L. Smolar, "Aaron, Jeroboam, and the Golden Calves," *JBL* 86 [1967] 137-138). Noth (*Exodus*, 200-201) and Coats (*Rebellion*, 184) see a tension in v 5, "and Aaron saw," as though he had not made the calf himself. Rather, "see" here means "perceive" and refers to the general situation as well as to the impious words uttered by the Israelites in v 4 (cf. Jer 2:31 [MT]— "Behold the word of Yahweh"). Beyerlin (pp. 24-25) claims that Moses learns of the rebellion in both vv 7-8 and 17-18; in fact, Joshua is informed by Moses in the latter passage. Beyerlin (p. 19) also sees duplicate intercessions in vv 11-14 and 30-32. Rather, the subject of the two dialogues is different. In the first, Moses appeases (*ḥlh*) Yahweh when the deity announces his intention to destroy all Israel and begin anew with Moses. Moses refuses the offer and persuades Yahweh to relent; the entire people will not perish. In the second, Moses, apparently nervous that divine vengeance might get out of hand after all, attempts to expiate (*kpr*), i.e., remove the *ḥaṭā'â* that clings to the people. Moses ascends that mountain with doubts (*'ûlay*, v 30) which prove justified, as Yahweh refuses his ultimatum (vv 32-33) on the principle that only the guilty may suffer for their sins. Thereby Yahweh again binds himself to punish only the guilty among the people, rather than blotting out the nation, which may have been Moses' intent from the start. While there is a slight overlap, it is in my opinion insufficient to prove that the accounts are duplicates (cf. Driver, *Exodus*, 355). One could better argue that the second intercession presupposes the first, that Moses offers his life precisely because he knows that Yahweh values him more than Israel (v 10). As for the supposed Deuteronomic language of vv 7-14, the similarity to Deut 9:25-29 only indicates that D is paraphrasing E, as J. Loza ("Exode XXXII et la redaction JE," *VT* 23 [1973] 32-38) shows in detail. I do not, however, accept Loza's view that Exod 32:7-11 and Num 14:11-25 stem from the redactor of JE; why would R^{JE} say the same thing in different words twice? Rather this is a typical doublet, the Exodus text being Elohistic and the Numbers Yahwistic. Finally, there is supposed to be inconsistency in the matter of the punishment of Israel. In v 14 Yahweh decides not to destroy Israel. In v 20 the Israelites are made to drink the ashes of the calf, regarded by many since the Rabbinic period as an ordeal; see the summary of past views in P. Gradwohl, "Die Verbrennung des Jungstiers, Ex. 32,20," *TZ* 19

(1963) 50-51. In v 28 the Levites slaughter approximately 3000 Israelites. In v 34 Yahweh promises that someday he will punish the sinners, while in v 35 he seems to do so immediately. V 34 supposedly contains an additional inconsistency—how can both Aaron and the people be held responsible for making the calf? None of these is really a contradiction. We have already seen that in v 14 Yahweh does not forswear all punishment, just total punishment. There is no basis for the belief that v 20 records the administration of an ordeal (see Gradwohl), for the draught is not recorded as having had any effect. In the manner of the destruction of the bull we may have rather a stereotyped (since gold neither may be pulverized nor burned [Num 31:22]) image of total annihilation; see Loewenstamm, "The Making and Destruction of the Golden Calf," *Bib* 48 (1967) 481-490; L. G. Perdue, "The Making and Destruction of the Golden Calf—A Reply," *Bib* 54 (1973) 237-246; Loewenstamm, "The Making and Destruction of the Golden Calf—a Rejoinder," *Bib* 56 (1975) 330-343. The *drinking* of the ashes is difficult to account for by this theory, however; Loewenstamm and P. L. Watson ("Mot, the God of Death, at Ugarit and in the Old Testament" [Yale diss., 1970] 174-187) suggest it indicates total dispersion and compare the birds' eating the dead Môtu (*CTA* 6.2.35-37). O. Hvidberg-Hansen ("Die Vernichtung des goldenes Kalbs und der ugaritischen Ernteritus," *ActOr* 33 [1971] 5-46) carries the parallel even further to reconstruct a rite of desacralization of grain that is supposedly depicted in Exodus 32, though it is most difficult to see any connection with the context. W. H. Gispen (*Exodus* [Bible Student's Commentary; Grand Rapids: Zondervan, 1982] 297-298) suggests simply that Moses' intent in making the people drink is to ridicule their new god by showing that it could be imbibed; Naḥmanides more imaginatively conjectures that the people are intended to excrete the god. On the other hand, R. Dussaud (*Les origins canaanéens du sacrifice israelite*[2] [Paris: Presses Universitaires de France, 1941] 245) associates the destruction of the calf with the sin offering; the Israelites absorb the *ḥaṭā'â* and are then killed. This is an attractive explanation, and I would propose a similar interpretation. The dissolution of the ashes of a cow (admittedly, not a bull) in running water is known from the Priestly Code as a method of removing impurity (Numbers 19; cf. 8:7; 31:23). The Deuteronomic Code contains a comparable clause about killing a heifer (*'eglâ*) by a running *naḥal* to remove *miasma*. In P the water is sprinkled, not drunk, but I nevertheless suspect that in Exod 32:20 Moses is taking drastic measures to expiate the sin of the people, to remove the *ḥaṭā'â* (vv 21,30,32,34). Feeding, rather than sprinkling, is a way of bringing the water into more intimate contact with the defiled. The Levites' action is similarly not described as a sorting out of innocent and guilty; it is rather an emergency shedding of blood to appease a wrathful deity; cf. the quick action of Pinehas in Num 25:7-8, which stops a plague, or the function of the blood in Exod 4:24-26. Moses' actions are a stopgap, but he must also expiate (*kpr*, v 30) in person. He fails to win full pardon, however, for Yahweh promises to punish the guilty in the future. To inform the reader that Yahweh was true to his word, the narrator adds an appropriate note in v 34; perhaps it refers to the later tribulations of Israel; see below, pp. 90-91, n. 146. Finally, while it is slightly surprising that both Aaron and the people are held accountable for the calf, he did make it at their instance. One final contradiction is noted by Holzinger (*Exodus*, 108)—the people remove their rings in Exod 32:2-3,24, yet once more remove their finery in 33:4. But why equate *n*^{e}*zāmîm* and *ʿădî*? On the contrary, the latter seems to be a more comprehensive term. The author may be creating a parallelism between the people's removal of their rings to commit apostasy and their more drastic removal of all finery in contrition (and perhaps in order to build the Tabernacle).

[129]Dtr describes the destruction of forbidden cult objects in a similar fashion (1 Kgs 15:13; 2 Kgs 23:4,6,12)—they are cast into the *Naḥal Qidrôn*; see Perdue, "Making and Destruction," 243. In these passages the wadi is dry.

[130]MT omits "and." The prior word, *ʿibrû* ends in *wāw*, and so either reading could be correct, both dittography and haplography being possible.

[131]G adds *autois*.

[132]The remainder of the verse is obscure. MT *milʾû yedkem* is slightly ungrammatical; we must read either **milʾî*, **mall*^{e}*ʾû* or **y*^{e}*dêkem*. We expect, however, after such a command to find detailed instructions on how the Levites are to consecrate themselves and a notation that they did so. G, on the other hand, has *eplērōsate tas cheiras hymōn*, "you filled your hands." The plural noun is not troublesome, since in defective orthography both singular and plural would appear *ydkm*. The difference in verbal form is harder to account for, however. Did the G *Vorlage* really have **mallē(ʾ)tem*, or is the Greek translation simply interpretive? The latter seems more plausible. It may be, in fact, that neither reading is correct and that we should read **māl*^{e}*ʾû* (or **mull*^{e}*ʾû*) *y*^{e}*dēkem*, "your hands have become full," i.e., you have been consecrated. Such a reading captures the sense of the Greek and yet respects the Hebrew consonantal text. We could also emend

slightly to an infinitive absolute *mālō'* (or *mallē'*), supposing that the final *wāw* of the MT is a dittography of the *yôd* of the following word.

133 G has nothing corresponding to *kî*. If we ignore the word, we can translate the verse smoothly, "You have become consecrated to Yahweh today, each by means of his son and his brother," i.e., by their deaths, as if they were inaugural offerings (McNeile, *Exodus*, 208-209). The killing of sons was not commanded in v 27, but cf. Deut 33:9. Most likely we have here an example of emphatic *kî* (McNeile, 208).

134 The sense of the preposition *b*[e]- is uncertain here. The *bêt* is best regarded, if the text is complete (see next note), as either the instrumental *bêt* or the *bêt pretii*; see Gunneweg, *Leviten*, 32.

135 If *kî* is the conjunction "for," something like **šālaḥ yādô* must be supplied here.

136 MT has "and to set," but this is difficult to make sense of. Probably the *wāw* is a dittography of the final letter of *'āḥîw*. G reflects no *wāw*.

137 *Mose*, 212 n. 1. Deut 13:7-12 is an instructive parallel, since it mandates the summary execution of any apostate, be it brother, son, daughter, wife or friend (*rēa'*).

138 Cf. Exod 2:1.

139 Apparently, D regards Aaron's life as one of the items under negotiation in Exod 32:31-34, since he bears primary responsibility for the sin of the people. The peculiar wording of v 33 may have been taken by D, perhaps correctly, as a pointed reference to Aaron.

140 Driver, *Exodus*, 355.

141 Loewenstamm ("*Hannûšḥâ 'bā'ēt hahî'' bin'ûmê happ*[e]*tîḥâ šel sēper d*[e]*bārîm*," *Tarbiz* 38 [1968-9] 99-104) views all cases of "at that time," including Deut 10:8-9, as additions; it is hard to see how in these cases we can distinguish an interpolation from a digression, however. Even if Loewenstamm is right, it is likely that the interpolator did not have the even later vv 6-7 before him, but wished to locate the ordination of the Levites at Horeb.

142 The equivalence of Sinai/Horeb and Canaan would have been especially clear if, as many suspect, the traditions took shape as covenant rituals performed in Canaan. See G. von Rad, "Das formgeschichtliche Problem des Hexateuch" (1938), *Gesammelte Studien zum Alten Testament* (Theologische Bücherei 8; Munich: Kaiser, 1958) 9-86.

143 The connection of covenant, sustenance and apostasy is also found in Psalm 81 and Exod 15:23-26.

144 On the tradition of the battle at the divine mountain, see Clifford, *Mountain*, 142-153. The practice of brandishing a pole as either a

magical act or a military signal (Josh 8:18,26) is reflected in both *CTA* 4.7.41, where Ba'lu wields a cedar (*'arz*, cf. *'ṣ brq* in *Ug5* 3.4) and in Exod 17:9-12; note that in Exod 17:16 Yahweh is said to personally war against Amalek. In Exod 17:8-16 the threatening gesture is somewhat incongruously combined with that of supplication, on whose iconography see Zenger, *Israel am Sinai*, 100-107.

145 On this motif in Canaan and Israel, see Clifford, *Mountain*, 112, 177-176.

146 Aberbach and Smolar ("Aaron, Jeroboam,") Childs (*Exodus*, 359-360), R. E. Clements (*Exodus* [Cambridge Bible Commentary; Cambridge: University, 1972] 206-207), Coats (*Rebellion*, 185), Cross (*Canaanite Myth*, 198-200) Driver (*Exodus*, 348-349), Holzinger (*Exodus*, 110), McNeile (*Exodus*, 204). Both Aaron and Jeroboam fashion molten, golden calves (Exod 32:4; 1 Kgs 12:28), and virtually identical statements are made before the statues (Exod 32:4; 1 Kgs 12:28). Strikingly, Exodus uses the plural, though there is but one bull; the reference is to the twin bulls of Israel. Aaron and Jeroboam each build an altar and proclaim a *ḥag* (Exod 32:5; 1 Kgs 12:32-33). The acts of both are described as *ḥaṭṭā(')t/ḥăṭā'â*. Both cults are ultimately expunged through slaughter (Exod 32:27; 1 Kgs 13:2; cf. 2 Kgs 23:16). The Levites are ordained in Exod 32:29, whereas Jeroboam appoints non-Levitic priests (1 Kgs 12:31) The polemic is unmistakable; Exod 32:34 seems to promise eventual punishment for any who worship golden calves (see Eissfeldt, *Einleitung*, 268-269). Yet there is a non-polemical strain, often overlooked, though it is not unexpected in an Elohistic (i.e., northern) text. The two intercession scenes (Exod 32:11-14, 30-32; cf. Jer 15:1) are also directed at the cults of Dan and Bethel, promising pardon to those who repudiate the golden calves and their priesthood. Nevertheless, the story ends with broken tablets, i.e., no Horeb covenant (cf. Hammurapi Code 37 [Borger, *Lesestücke* 2, 14] or the shattered tablets described in D. J. Wiseman, *The Vassal-Treaties of Esarhaddon* [London: Harrison, 1958] i), although the patriarchal covenant stands (Exod 33:1). It is inconceivable, however, that E considered the Horeb covenant void. It may be that, in a passage omitted by R^{JE}, E told of a covenant renewal; Eissfeldt ("Lade und Stierbild," *ZAW* 58 [1940-1] 191) shows that there probably is a large lacuna before *mēhar Ḥōrēb* in Exod 33:6. Alternatively, the Elohist's point may have been that there was no valid covenant *since Jeroboam*. At any rate, when J and E were combined in the south, the redactor did create a scene of covenant restoration (Exod 33:12-34:28) which, like his very act of combining

J and E, invited northern refugees to return to Jerusalemite Yahwism; note that Jer 31:31, too, speaks of a new covenant in the context of the reunification of the kingdom. The work of R^{JE} was a remarkable act of conciliation, inasmuch as the refugees were hardly in a position to demand that Judah change its Torah. That there was a period of admiration for northern traditions in Judah is also evident in D and Dtr.

[147]It is impossible that the bulls of the North were associated with any god but Yahweh; see Cross, *Canaanite Myth*, 74. On the statues as pedestals see, *inter alios*, Noth *Geschichte Israels*[5] (Göttingen: Vandenhoeck & Ruprecht, 1963) 212-213.

[148]Suggested orally by B. Halpern.

[149]Isa 44:9-20; Jer 10:1-10; Ps 115:4-8.

[150]See Eissfeldt, "Lade," Beyerlin, *Sinaitraditionen*, 144-153 and Cross, *Canaanite Myth*, 74.

[151]We are not told that Jeroboam displaced any priests, but rather installed new ones.

[152]Exod 17:2-18:27; 192b (*wayyiḥan*)-9, 16b (*wayhî qōlōt*)-17, 19; 20:18-24:14b (*hahar*), 18b (*wayhî*); 32:1-33:11.

[153]Exod 24:1-2, 9-11, as opposed to 3-8; see Beyerlin, *Sinaitraditionen*, 19-23.

[154]On this form see Coats, *Rebellion*, 29-43. For a survey of interpretation see Childs, *Exodus*, 254-264. Childs's own treatment is the most persuasive; he attributes the stereotypical features to an oral stage of transmission and views the rebellion tales as general homiletic material, not, *pace* Coats (*Rebellion*) and Fritz (*Wüste*), as directed against any particular situation. My only disagreement with Childs is on source attribution; I consider most of the murmuring stories Elohistic.

[155]Two aspects of the Massah-Meribah tradition remain unaccounted for in this treatment. First, the forty years of Ps 95:10-11 are not mentioned by E, though we might have expected them in the aftermath of the golden calf. Perhaps it was in Eissfeldt's missing matter in Exod 33:6. Friedman (*Exile*, 107) posits that Joshua is disassociated from the golden calf affair precisely to allow him to enter the land; if this is correct, it suggests that death in the wilderness was decreed at this juncture. But we should not attempt to harmonize away all difficulties, since any telling may omit particular features found in other versions.

The other loose end is the inconsistency of who tests whom. In Deut 33:8-11 Yahweh tests the Levites. In Ps 81:8 Yahweh tests the Israelites, who apparently fail. In Exod 17:2,7; Deut 6:16 and Ps 95:9 Israel tests Yahweh. There is similar lack of agreement as to strife; does Yahweh strive with Levi (Deut 33:8) or does Israel strive with Moses (Exod 17:2)? As long as two parties conflict either can be said to be testing and striving with the other, and so this aspect of the tradition, etiologically motivated, is fluid.

156 Signs of priestly authorship are the terms *'ēdâ* (v 2,8) and *gāwa'* (v 3), the presence of Aaron beside Moses (vv 2,6,8,10,12), their falling on their faces (cf. Num 14:5; 16:4,22), the advent of the Glory (cf. Num 14:10; 16:19; 17:7), the stress upon the power of the word (cf. Genesis 1) and the importance of sanctification. Also, the Tent seems to be in the center of the camp. Virtually all modern commentators see this text as the result of either the amalgamation of several sources or a complex process of literary accretion. See Cornill, "Beiträge," 20-34; Gray, *Numbers*, 258-259; G. Hölscher, "Zu Num 20:1-13," *ZAW* 45 (1927) 239-240; Noth, *Das vierte Buch Mose. Numeri* (ATD 7; Göttingen: Vandenhoeck & Ruprecht, 1966) 127-129; J. de Vaulx, *Les Nombres* (Sources Bibliques; Paris: Gabalda, 1972) 223. Coats (*Rebellion*, 71-82) and F. Kohata ("Die priesterschriftliche Uberlieferungsgeschichte von Numeri XX 1-13," *Annual of the Japanese Biblical Institute* 3 [1977] 3-34) maintain (correctly) that our text is entirely P, but attribute supposed unevenness to preliterary tradition. M. Margaliot ("*Ḥēṭ(') Mōše(h) wᵉ'ahărôn bᵉmê Mᵉrîbâ,*" *Beth Mikra* 19 [1974] 374-400) and Budd (*Numbers*, 216-217) stress rather the lack of unevenness, as would I. The best evidence of conflation is in vv 2-5, yet nothing is actually said twice (except *lamâ* and *hazze(h)*) in vv 4 and 5. Rather, there is artistry; the people's complaint moves backward through time—would we had died with Korah, why are we in this desert, why did you bring us out of Egypt at all—while the description of the lack of water grows ever more graphic—no water for people (v 2), none for cattle (v 4), none even for vegetation (v 5)—finishing with "there was no water to drink," echoing "there was no water for the community" (v 2). As in Exod 17:2-3, the effect of growing hysteria is effectively achieved.

157 On this aspect of the priestly work, see Friedman, *Exile*, 44-119, *passim*. On the sin of Moses, see my "Rod."

158 G translates freely, on the analogy of Exod 17:3, as though the Hebrew were **lᵉhāmît 'ōtānû* (*šām* is not rendered).

159 G "is not sown."

160 MT singular; G plural. MT is preferable as the *lectio difficilior*, but it is hard to be confident.

161 G "Yahweh."

162 G adds "to me."

163 So G; MT "his," under the influence of *yādô* and other references to Moses' rod. The staff in this story is Aaron's; see Propp, "Rod."

[164]Not reflected in G.

[165]Other priestly passages that allude to this incident are Num 20:24; 27:14; Deut 32:51.

[166]So Seebass, *Mose und Aaron*, 65.

[167]See H. G. May, "Some Cosmic Connotations of *Mayim Rabbîm*, 'Many Waters'," *JBL* 74 (1955) 9-21.

[168]Elsewhere, P uses the compound name Meribath-Kadesh (Num 27:14; Deut 32:51), in which he is followed by Ezek 47:19; 48:28 (G).

[169]See Budd, *Numbers*, 219.

[170]See the critical comments of de Vaux, *Histoire ancienne d'Israël* (2 vols.; Paris: Lecoffre, 1971-3) 392-397 and P. Buis, "Qadesh, un lieu maudit," *VT* 24 (1974) 268-285. The latter stresses that the connection of the spy and Meribah accounts with Kadesh are not reflective of ancient tradition, but an innovation of P deserving consideration as such.

Chapter Four
RESTORATION

This chapter will examine references in later, especially exilic, literature to the Water in the Wilderness motif studied above. That such allusions are common in prophecies of return from exile is not surprising, given the motif's dual associations with sustenance in times of hardship and the fertility of Canaan. The themes of rebellious ingratitude or apostasy, inappropriate in consolatory texts, do not appear.

Jeremiah

The earliest known prophet to predict a second journey through the desert corresponding to that of the days of Moses, often called (with slight inaccuracy)[1] the Second Exodus motif,[2] was Jeremiah. Earlier, Hosea had prophesied a return to the desert and a reestablishment of the covenant (2:16-22), but there was no Exodus, no escape from bondage, because there had, as yet, been no exile. After 722/1, however, Jeremiah expressed hope for a new departure from captivity.

> *14*Behold, days are coming, word of Yahweh, when it will no longer be said[3] "As Yahweh lives, who took the children of Israel from the land of Egypt," *15*but rather "As Yahweh lives, who took the house[4] of Israel from a northern land and from all the lands into which he had expelled them and brought them back to their land, which he[5] had given their fathers" (Jer 16:14-15; cf. 23:7-8).

We cannot tell if Jeremiah speaks of the exile of the northern kingdom or of the southern, whether anticipated or experienced. Jer 31:1-22, on the other hand, clearly describes the return of the exiles of northern Israel in language referring to the departure from Egypt and journey to Canaan, although these words were early interpreted as referring to the Judean exiles as well.[6]

Chapter 31 (G 38) contains two descriptions of the return of Ephraim to Canaan and to Jerusalemite suzerainty. Vv 2-6 tell of Yahweh coming upon Israel's refugees wandering in the desert. Yahweh falls in love and promises that joy and prosperity will return to the Israelites, that Ephraim will once again be inhabited and subject to Zion. Vv 7-14 say much the same thing:[7]

*7*For thus says Yahweh:
Sing to[8] Jacob in joy,[9]
Shout at the head of the nations.
Proclaim, exult and say,
"Yahweh has saved his people,[10]
The remnant of Israel."
*8*Behold, I bring them from the northern land;[11]
I gather them from the corners of the earth,
Among them the blind and the halt,[12]
Pregnant and birthing together.[13]
A great crowd will return.
Behold,[14] *9*in weeping they will come,[15]
Though I will lead them with compassion.[16]
I will guide them to brooks of water[17]
In a straight road in which they will not falter.[18]
For I am Israel's father,
And Ephraim is my firstborn.
*10*Hear, O nations, the word of Yahweh
And tell it among the distant isles.
Say, "Israel's disperser will gather her
And guard her as a shepherd his flock."[19]
*11*For Yahweh has ransomed Jacob
And redeemed him from a hand too strong for him.
*12*They will come singing to Zion's height,
Flowing toward the bounty of Yahweh,
Toward the grain,[20] toward the wine, toward the oil,[21]
Toward the cattle, large and small.
Their throats[22] will be like a moist garden;[23]
They will not travail further.
*13*Then will the lass dance merrily,
The young man and the old together.[24]
I will change their mourning to joy;
I will console[25] them and cheer them from their grief.
*14*I shall moisten[26] the throats of the priests with fat,[27]

> And my people will be sated with my bounty.
> Word of Yahweh.

Many features of this oracle are characteristic of the prophecies of Second Isaiah dealing with the Judean restoration, some of which are examined below. We have the address to the nations, the march of the invalids,[28] the journey in a flock[29] along a road through the desert to Zion,[30] restoration of fertility.[31] For our purposes, the most important element is the guidance to water, a pastoral image evocative of Yahweh's leading Israel from oasis to oasis. While the fertility of Canaan is prominently featured, it is not associated with the provision of water, whose function is simply to assuage thirst.

Ezekiel

Ezek 20:33-40 likewise describes of a new journey out of exile through the desert, but the references to the Mosaic period are more explicit, and, of course, Ezekiel is now speaking of the entire people of Israel, not just the northern refugees.

> 33 As[32] I live, says my lord, I will rule you with a
> strong hand, with an extended arm and with poured
> out wrath. 34 I will bring you out from among the
> peoples and gather you from the lands in which you
> have been scattered with a strong hand, with an
> extended arm and with poured out wrath. 35 I will
> bring you to the wilderness of the peoples, and there I
> will enter into judgment with you, face to face. 36 As
> I entered into judgment with your ancestors in the
> wilderness of Egypt, so will I enter into judgment[33]
> with you—word of my lord Yahweh.[34] 37 I will make
> you pass under the[35] rod and muster you.[36] 38 I will
> purge the rebels and sinners against me[37] from you; I
> will take them from the land of their sojourn, but they
> will not come[38] to the soil of Israel, so that you will
> know that I am Yahweh. 39 As for you, house of
> Israel, thus says my lord Yahweh: Let each go after
> his abominations and worship[39] another,[40] if you will
> not heed me, but never again defile my holy name
> with your offerings and abominations. 40 But on my

> holy mountain, the mountain of the height of Israel[41]—word of my lord God—there the whole house of Israel will serve me in the land;[42] there will I receive them[43] with favor; there will I seek your offerings and the best of your sacrifices, of all that you consecrate.

The expressions "with a strong hand and an extended arm" are evocative of the Exodus,[44] and the judgment in the desert, "face to face," is comparable with the experience of Moses.[45] The pastoral imagery is more pronounced than in Jer 31:9, but there is no reference to water. The tradition of rebellion and punishment in the desert is known to the prophet, however, as we also see earlier in the chapter.

The goal of the journey is clearly Mount Zion. W. Zimmerli[46] and J. D. Levenson[47] view this description of a "Second Exodus" as prefatory to the legislation of chaps. 40-48, which parallel the laws of Sinai. Ezekiel's description of Mount Zion in 47:1-12 is noteworthy, since it refers to miraculous waters flowing in the desert.

> *1*He returned me to the door of the Temple, and water
> was running eastward from under the threshold of the
> Temple, for the Temple faced east, and the water was
> emerging from the southern side[48] of the Temple,[49]
> south of the altar. *2*He led me out by way of the gate,
> northwards,[50] and took me around the outer way to
> the gate of the court,[51] which faced east, and there
> was water[52] dripping from the southern side. *3*When
> the man came eastward,[53] a line in his hand, he meas-
> ured a thousand with the cubit[54] and made me pass[55]
> through the water: it was foot-deep[56] water. *4*He
> measured a thousand cubits and made me cross the
> water: knee-deep water,[57] and he measured a
> thousand cubits and made me cross: hip-deep water.
> *5*He measured a thousand; there was a brook[58] I[59]
> could not cross, for the waters were high, requiring
> swimming,[60] an uncrossable brook. *6*He said to me,
> "Have you seen, human?" and took me back[61] to the
> bank of the brook. *7*When he returned me[62] there
> was on the bank of the brook a very big tree[63] on
> each side. *8*He said to me, "This water is going

> towards the eastern territory and will descend into the Arabah and come to the sea, the polluted[64] water,[65] and the water will be healed. *9*Every living thing that crawls to wherever the brook[66] goes will revive, and there will be very much fish, for this water will have arrived, and they will be healed[67] and revive. Any place the brook reaches will revive.[68] *10*Fishermen from En Gedi and En Eglaim will stand by it; it will be[69] a place for spreading nets. Of every sort will be their[70] fish, like the fish of the Mediterranean, very numerous. *11*Its swamps[71] and pits[72] will not be healed, but will be made into salt. *12*By the brook, on each bank, on either side, will rise every kind of fruit tree. Its leaf[73] will not wither nor its fruit cease, but it will bear for months,[74] since its water will come from the Temple, and its fruit will be[75] for food and its leaf[76] for medicine."

This is the climax of the prophecy of Ezekiel. The motif of the life-giving waters of Zion derives from the Canaanite descriptions of the abode of 'Ilu discussed above.[77] Since Ezekiel associates the mountain of Zion with Eden in chaps. 28 and 31, it is not surprising to find paradisiacal motifs pertaining to Zion in chap. 47.[78] We should also consider the possibility, however, that Ezekiel was familiar with the tradition that a special mountain in the desert, identified by E with the site of the lawgiving, was a source of water. Even if he was not, his bringing together the Eden, Zion and Sinai traditions is an instructive parallel to the manner in which the Elohist brought together the themes of Water in the Wilderness and the Divine Mountain.

Second Isaiah

Unlike Jeremiah and Ezekiel, Second Isaiah makes explicit reference to the Water in the Wilderness tradition, using vocabulary familiar to us from our study of the pre-exilic texts. He, too, speaks of a new march through the desert, and, like Ezekiel, he makes reference to the primordial paradise. The association of the events of Creation, Exodus and Restoration is typical of this prophet, as 51:9-11 demonstrates:

9 Awake, awake,[79] put on strength,
O Arm of Yahweh!
Awake as in days of yore,
The beginning of time.
10 Was it not you who hacked[80] Rahab,
Impaled the Serpent;[81]
Was it not you who attacked/dried[82] the sea,
The waters of the great deep,
Who turned[83] the depths of the sea into a road
For the redeemed to cross?
11 The ransomed[84] of Yahweh will return
And enter Zion in song
With eternal joy upon their head.[85]
Exultation and joy will overtake them;[86]
Grief[87] and groaning will flee.[88]

Second Isaiah treats the Water in the Wilderness theme in much the same way, mixing references to Creation, the Mosaic period and his own time. In 48:20-21, he refers only to the wilderness wanderings, but there is deliberate ambiguity; the prophet speaks of both the immediate future and the nation's distant past.

20 Leave Babylon!
Flee the Chaldeans!
Tell it with a jubilant voice.
Say this;
Send it to the ends of the earth;
Say:[89]
Yahweh has redeemed Jacob, his slave.
21 They did not thirst[90]
When he led them through the wastes.[91]
He made water flow from a mountain [*ṣûr*] for them
And cleft the mountain [*ṣûr*], so that water gushed.[92]

Here the prophet seeks to assuage the doubts of those who dread the desert's rigors, predicting a duplication of the Mosaic miracle.[93]

In 49:8-13 Second Isaiah speaks of the return from captivity. The deity does not miraculously produce the water, but only leads to it. Nevertheless, there is allusion to the days of Moses, when Israel roamed from oasis to oasis.

*8*Thus says Yahweh:
In a favorable time I have answered you;
In a day of victory I have helped you.
I have guarded[94] you and made you into a covenant
of a nation[95]
To rebuild[96] the land,
To acquire ruined properties,
*9*To say to the prisoners, "Come forth,"
To those in darkness, "Show yourselves."
They will graze by the roads;[97]
On all the barren heights[98] will be their pasture.
*10*They will neither hunger nor thirst;
Neither heat nor sun will strike them,
For he who pities them guides them.
He leads them to fountains of water.
*11*I will make all my[99] mountains into a road,
And my highways will be raised up.[100]
*12*Look, these come from afar,
Look, these from the north and the west,[101]
And these from the land of Syene.[102]
*13*Sing, O heavens, and rejoice, O earth;
O mountains, burst[103] into song,
For Yahweh has consoled his people
And pitied its wretches.

Both Isa 48:20-21 and 49:8-12 are based upon Jeremiah 31.[104] We have similar commands to proclaim that Yahweh has saved or redeemed Israel/Jacob (Jer 31:7,11; Isa 48:20). Isa 49:10 paraphrases Jer 31:9, making the pastoral imagery more pronounced. Compare the use of the participle *m*^{e}*zāre(h)* in Jer 31:10 with *m*^{e}*raḥamām* in Isa 49:10. Finally, Jer 31:21 refers to the *m*^{e}*sillâ* by which Ephraim departed and on which it is expected to return, while Isa 49:11 also speaks of a *derek/m*^{e}*sillâ*.

Isa 43:16-20 contrasts the deeds of Yahweh in the days of Moses and in his own time. Yahweh will make a new thing, but it will correspond closely to his past acts.

*16*Thus says Yahweh,
Who makes a way in the sea,
A road in the mighty waters,
*17*Who brings forth[105] chariotry and horse,
Soldier and warrior together.[106]

They lie down, never to rise;
They die down and go out like [smoldering] flax.[107]
*18*Do not remember the former things,
And do not consider ancient events.
*19*Now I am about to make a new thing;[108]
Now it sprouts. Do you not know it?
I will make a way in the desert
And roads[109] in the wilderness.
*20*The wild beasts will honor me,
Jackals and ostriches,
For I will have produced water in the desert
And rivers in the wilderness,
To give drink to my chosen people.
*21*Let the people I created for myself
Tell of my praise-worthy deed.

Just as once Yahweh made a way in the Red Sea, so now he will make a road in the desert. Moreover, a contrast is implied between the drying of the sea and the moistening of the desert. Note that the water, whose purpose is to water the people, is described as rivers, which apparently benefit also the jackals and ostriches, the customary symbols of sterility and desolation. Here is a hint of the fertility theme we discussed in chapter two. The intent is again to encourage potential returnees to brave the wilderness.

The theme of fertility is pronounced in Isa 41:17-20, which speaks of the conversion of the desert into a paradise.

*17*The poor and the destitute[110] seek water, but there is none;
Their tongue is parched with thirst.
I, Yahweh,[111] will answer them;
I, the god of Israel, will not abandon them.
*18*I will open up rivers on the barren heights
And springs within the valleys;
I will make the desert a watery swamp[112]
And the thirsty land water sources.
*19*I will place in the desert cedar,[113]
Acacia, myrtle and olive;
I will put in the wilderness juniper,
Box tree and cypress[114] together,
*20*That they may see and know,
That they may both pay heed and consider

> That the hand of Yahweh has done this,[115]
> And that the holy one of Israel has created it.[116]

This oracle has contact with Ps 114 in both theme and in the phrase *'ăgam-mayim* (Isa 41:18; Ps 114:8), and it corroborates the exegesis of the latter as pertaining to fertility. Yahweh's response to the thirst of the desert wanderers is not just to provide drinking water, but to perform an act of creation (*br'*, v 20), planting a garden in the desert. In this text the miracle of Water in the Wilderness is clearly linked with fertility and creation.

Isaiah 35[117] is similar to 41:17-20, in that it portrays the conversion of the desert into a garden. The subject of the oracle is a march through the desert to Zion.

> *1*Let the desert and the parched land[118] exult;[119]
> Let the wilderness rejoice and blossom.
> Like a *ḥăbaṣṣelet*-flower[120] *2*let it bloom;
> Let it rejoice and sing out in joy.[121]
> It shall be given the glory of Lebanon,
> The[122] splendor of Carmel and Sharon.[123]
> These[124] will see the glory of Yahweh,
> The splendor of our god.[125]
> *3*Strengthen[126] the limp hands,
> Invigorate the faltering knees;
> *4*Tell[127] the fainthearted: "Take heart; fear not."
> Behold, your[128] god avenges;[129]
> The retribution of God comes;[130]
> It/He comes to save you.[131]
> *5*Then the eyes of the blind will see,
> And the ears of the deaf will be opened.[132]
> *6*Then the lame will prance like a stag,
> And the tongue of the dumb will sing.[133]
> For water sources will be cleft open in the desert,
> And brooks[134] in the arid land.
> *7*The parched ground will become a swamp,[135]
> And the sere land fountains[136] of water,
> In the abode[137] of jackals[138] a bog,[139]
> Grass[140] will become reed and rush.
> *8*A highway and a way[141] will[142] be there;
> It[143] will be called the Holy Way.
> No one unclean will pass on it;
> The redeemed will walk in it;
> The dispersed will not stray.[144]

The frivolous will not wander.
9 There will be no lion there;
No wild beast will mount it[145]
...will not be found there.[146]
The redeemed will walk in it.[147]
10 The ransomed of Yahweh will return
And enter Zion in song
With eternal joy upon their head.
Exaltation and joy will overtake them;
Grief and groaning will flee.[148]

The desert through which the returnees march is converted into a paradise, complete with absence of wild animals.[149] The goal of the journey is Yahweh's holy mountain, Zion. Notice that Second Isaiah, like Jeremiah, speaks of a march of invalids, but here they are actually healed,[150] just as Yahweh heals the desert of its sterility; we may also compare the association of the Water in the Wilderness with healing in Exod 15:26 and Ezek 47:8-12, as well as in "Enki and Ninhursag."[151]

Second Isaiah also uses the motif of irrigation to describe the salutary effects of Yahweh's justice and word in 44:1-4; 45:8 and 55:10-13.

1 Now hear, Jacob my slave,[152]
Israel, whom I have chosen.
2 Thus says Yahweh, who made you;[153]
He who formed you in the womb, who aids you.[154]
Fear not, Jacob, my slave.[155]
Jeshurun,[156] whom I have chosen.
3 For (as) I pour out water upon the thirsty,
Torrents upon the dry ground.[157]
(So)[158] I will pour my spirit upon your seed
And my blessing upon your progeny.
4 They will flourish as[159] a verdant *bîn*-tree,[160]
As poplars along water courses.

Drip,[161] heavens above;
Let the clouds shed[162] righteousness.
Let the earth open[163] and let victory blossom,[164]
Let it sprout[165] righteousness too.
I, Yahweh, have created it (45:8).

> *10*For[166] just as the rain and snow fall from the sky
> and do not return thither[167] without watering the
> earth, so that it bear and sprout, giving seed to the
> sower and bread to the eater, *11*so will be my word,
> which will proceed from my mouth—it will not return
> to me unfulfilled, but rather it will accomplish what-
> ever I desire[168] and achieve its mission. *12*For in joy
> will you go forth, and in peace will you be led.[169]
> The mountains and hills will break out in song before
> you, and all trees of the field will clap their hands.
> *13*Instead[170] of the thorn, the cypress will rise, and,
> instead of the bramble, the myrtle will rise. It will be
> a memorial for Yahweh, an eternal sign that will not
> be cut down (55:10-13).

Considered superficially, Second Isaiah's use of the Water in the Wilderness theme seems to have been designed to allay fears of the arduous journey through the Syrian steppe. Yet he prophesied not only of drinking water, but of the blooming of the desert, a recapitulation of Genesis 2.[171] Second Isaiah was a visionary and may have expected such things to happen, but he was a pragmatist as well; he was trying to encourage people to return to Judah.[172]

Reasons for staying in Babylon were numerous and persuasive for many of the Jews. They had been living for half a century in Mesopotamia, some apparently comfortably, as Jeremiah had advised (29:4-7).[173] The desert was poor in sustenance for human or animal and probably haunted by marauders.[174] The land that was the goal of the journey had declined in the chaotic years after 586.[175] Second Isaiah, in his extant oracles, addressed some of these concerns—pricipally, as we have seen, that of the sterility of the desert.

The exuberance of his language suggests that he expected more than the healing of the desert. Why should this have been a concern to the Jews at all? One facet is that allusions to creation in these and other Deutero-Isaianic passages[176] is a way of describing the "re-creation" of the people. One of the oldest traceable motifs of Israelite literature is the identification of the formation of the people with the events of creation.[177]

Such an analysis, while valid, skips a step. The main interest of a creation story is often to assure the listener of the gods' control over the universe and ability to supply basic requirements such as fertility. I have shown that the motif of Water in the Wilderness served this same function for the Israelites, hence its popularity. While not at all denying other, less mundane interpretations of Second Isaiah's emphasis on creation and the healing of the desert, I think we must not overlook the practical aspects of his message. By employing to the Water in the Wilderness motif, he foretold the restoration of fertility to Canaan. If Yahweh can heal the Syrian desert, how much more easily can he heal his holy land? The key to this aspect of Second Isaiah's prophecy is 51:3:

> For Yahweh has comforted Zion,[178]
> Comforted all her ruins.
> He will make[179] her desert like Eden
> And her wasteland like the garden of Yahweh.[180]
> Joy and gladness will be found in it,[181]
> Gratitude and the sound of song.

Psalm 107

As argued above,[182] Psalms 106-107 form a triptych, being independent yet interrelated. Together they present a synopsis of Israelite history—Yahweh's acts of kindness to the patriarchs and the generation of the Exodus (Psalm 105); Israel's repeated insurrection, for which it was punished with exile (Psalm 106); Yahweh's relenting and the return of Israel (Psalm 107).

All three poems refer to the Exile, even Psalm 105, which ostensibly deals only with harmony between Yahweh and Israel. It stresses the inviolability of the patriarchs, called "prophets" and "anointed ones" (v 15), as they wandered from "nation to nation, from kingdom to another people" (v 13); such language fits better the international situation of the middle first millennium than the tales of migration in Genesis. Similarly, the story of Joseph's imprisonment is embellished (v 18); compare Ps 107:10,14,16, which use prison as a metaphor for exile. The claim of Ps 105:19 that imprisonment "refined" Joseph is not based upon Genesis, but is rather an interpretation of the Babylonian captivity. The king, the "ruler of peoples" who frees Joseph from upon Genesis, but is rather an interpretation of the Babylonian captivity. The king, the "ruler of peoples" who frees Joseph from prison and sets him above the nobles of his house, is Cyrus as well as Pharaoh. The prospering of Israel in Egypt is parallel to its prosperity in Babylon. The main theme of this psalm is the promise of Canaan to Abraham and his descendants (vv 8-11, 42), a commitment still binding in the psalmist's day. Taken alone, the psalm cannot be dated precisely; it could belong to the exilic or post-exilic periods.

Psalm 106, also basing itself upon old, written texts, presents a complementary view of Israelite history, stressing the people's neverending rebellion. The psalm is primarily an attempt to account for the Babylonian exile, foreshadowed in v 27 and perhaps 34-35. Yet the poet is not a pessimist, for he tells that Yahweh repeatedly relented, sometimes of his own volition (v 10), sometimes because of the intervention of human leaders (v 23, 30-31). Yahweh finally did punish the people with exile (vv 40-42), but there is hope: history suggests that Yahweh may once more forgive Israel (vv 43-46). Accordingly, the psalm concludes with a prayer for restoration (v 47). The work is apparently written from the perspective of the exile.

Psalm 107, the third panel of the triptych, tells of the fulfilment of the promises of Psalm 105 and of the reconciliation desired by Psalm 106.[183]

Praise Yah![184]
*1*Praise Yahweh, for[185] he is good,
For his fidelity is eternal.
*2*Let the redeemed of Yahweh so say,
Whom[186] he redeemed from the enemy's hand.
*3*From[187] lands he gathered them,
From east and west,
From[188] north and sea.[189]
*4*Those who wandered[190] in a desolate waste[191]
Could find no road to an inhabited city.
*5*Hungry and thirsty,
Their soul grew faint within them,
*6*So they cried to Yahweh when they were in distress;
From[192] their straits he rescued them.
*7*He led them in a straight road
To an inhabited city.

9For he sated the throbbing[194] throat,
And filled the hungry throat with plenty (Ps 107:1-9).

The Jews are seeking an inhabitable city (v 4), which they finally find in v 36, marching along the road (v 7) that is such a typical feature of the prophecies of restoration. Along the way Yahweh sustains the people with food and drink[195]. A description of liberation from prison follows (vv 10-16). The prison metaphor signifies not simply confinement, but rather deserved punishment (vv 11-17). The references to the darkness of the prison (vv 10,14) recall Second Isaiah (Isa 42:7; 49:9). V 18 graphically describes the inability of the ill to stomach food; they starve to death. They appeal to Yahweh (v 19) and are healed (v 20). This has no obvious reference either to departure from Egypt or from Babylon, though we might recall healing at Marah (Exod 15:26) and the healing promised to the returnees of Isa 35:5-6. Then the poet abruptly switches metaphor, describing the exile as a voyage in a storm-tossed ship. Notice how artfully he uses language evocative of theomachy and creation (v 24-25), traditionally associated with the Exodus, to introduce deceptively this innovative section. Yahweh saves not by stirring the sea with his winds, as in the Exodus, but by calming it. By implication, he has conquered the sea to save his people, just as, in a sense, he conquered the desert in vv 4-9 by sustaining them. This is made explicit in the following verses.

33He turns rivers into a desert,
Water sources into a thirsty place,
34A fruitful land into a salt flat,
Because of the turpitude of its inhabitants.
35He makes the desert a watery swamp [* *'ǎgam-mayim*],
The thirsty land water sources,[196]
36And settled[197] there the hungry,
And there they founded an inhabited city.
37They sowed fields and planted vineyards
And made a fruitful yield.
38He blessed them, and they multiplied greatly;
Their cattle did not diminish (vv 33-38).

As in Isa 42:15, Yahweh's power to cause sterility is also proclaimed. In contrast, the psalmist then recalls the Water in the

Wilderness theme, tying it most clearly to the fertility of Palestine. Note that the hunger and thirst of the Israelites (v 5) are twice assuaged. In v 9 it seems that they are fed in the desert, though v 7 associates the sustenance with the fertility of Palestine. In vv 35-38, they are again sated. That is, there is an identification of the sustenance in the desert and the fertility of Canaan, the former being emblematic of the latter, which is precisely what we have been arguing for the Water in the Wilderness theme throughout the Bible. The language is cryptic, imitative of Wisdom, as if the author interpreted the national story as containing a moral for individuals. Psalm 107 is written from the vantage of the restoration, as v 22 presupposes the presence of the Second Temple. Quotations of Third Isaiah and Job corroborate this date.[198] As for the set of Psalms 105-107, it would seem that the first two were written in exile and the last upon their author's return. The psalmist was apparently not among the first wave of returnees, since the Temple was already rebuilt.

Summary

Jeremiah was the first prophet to speak of a new journey out of exile, using language evocative of the Exodus and desert wanderings. He alludes to the provision of water, but, as in Gen 21:19, Yahweh leads to, rather than creates, water (Jer 31:9). The goal of the journey is Mount Zion, the source of agricultural bounty (vv 12-14). Ezekiel 20:33-44 also describes a new journey, but omits the gift of water in the desert. As in Jeremiah, the goal is Zion (v 40), in a sense analogous to Sinai-Horeb. Ezek 47:1-12 describes the bounty of Canaan as due to waters flowing from Zion.

Second Isaiah most clearly refers to the Water in the Wilderness motif in chap. 35; 41:17-20; 43:16-20; 48:20-21; 49:8-13, announcing, like the author of Psalms 105-107, his confidence in Yahweh's ability to sustain Israel in the Syrian desert, re-create the nation and restore the fertility of Canaan.

NOTES TO CHAPTER FOUR

[1]"Exodus" usually refers to the crossing of the Red Sea, yet the texts in question refer not only to the Exodus proper, but to water in the desert, the covenant, the journey to Canaan and the settlement of the land.

[2]See most recently K. Kiesow, *Exodustexte im Jesajabuch* (Orbis Biblicus et Orientalis 24; Göttingen: Vandenhoeck & Ruprecht, 1979).

[3]MT *yē'āmēr*; G reads **yō(')m*^{e}*rû* as in 23:7.

[4]So G, adopted here for maximum variance; MT has "children of Israel."

[5]Actually, the last two verbs are in the first person, as the prophet identifies himself with Yahweh, but I am unable to capture this in translation.

[6]It seems that the prose portions of Jeremiah 30-31 were composed after 587/6 and allude to the exile of Judah (30:3; 31:23); their association with the poetic oracles that deal chiefly, if not exclusively, with Ephraim (31:5-6,9,15,18,20) itself constitutes an interpretation of the latter.

[7]This passage has been denied to Jeremiah on account of its similarity to Second Isaiah by E. W. Nicholson (*The Book of the Prophet Jeremiah Chapters 26-52* [Cambridge Bible Commentary; Cambridge: University, 1975] 63). Any parallels, however, are *a priori* more likely to show Jeremiah's influence upon Second Isaiah. Moreover, as will be seen below, at times it seems that Second Isaiah is carrying forward the thoughts of Jeremiah.

[8]While the translation "Sing, O Jacob" is possible, it seems to me that the adressees are the nations of the world, as Freedman has argued in "The Structure of Isaiah 40:1-11," forthcoming in *Perspectives on Language and Text* (Fs. F. I. Andersen; ed. E. W. Conrad, E. G. Newing; Winona Lake, Indiana: Eisenbrauns). Note that Israel in the following verses is referred to in the third person.

[9]G reflects one word fewer than the MT. Most likely it omits *ronnû* and reads **śimḥû*. *L*^{e}*ya'ăqōb* is read with the prior line, yielding, "Thus says Yahweh to Jacob, 'Rejoice and shout at the head of nations'." It is difficult to choose between MT and G here.

[10]So G; MT has "save, O Yahweh, your people," which is not a song of joy, but of supplication.

[11]As in Jer 6:2, G omits "land." This yields more balanced cola, so perhaps the MT has anticipated *miyyark*^{e}*tê-'āreṣ*.

[12]G contains an interesting corruption of this verse, presupposing

**bmw'd psḥ*, "on the festival of Passover," for MT *bm 'wr wpsḥ*.

[13]G "and it will bear a great multitude," i.e., **w^{e}yōledet qāhāl gādôl*, makes no sense and must be a corruption of the MT reading.

[14]Reading, with *BHS*, **hinnē(h)* for MT *hēnnâ*.

[15]G has "they left," which makes a good antithesis to the second colon. Conceivably the original reading was **yāṣ^e'û*.

[16]So G, reading **tanḥûmîm*; MT *taḥănûnîm*, "supplications," seems inconsistent with the context. The tears the returnees shed must be those of joy, but the scribe who wrote *taḥănûnîm* interpreted them as of regret.

[17]G "residing [singular] by waters" is inexplicable.

[18]G "wander" is perhaps derived from Isa 35:8.

[19]It is not certain whether the quotation ends in here or at the end of v 14.

[20]G reads *'al-*'ereṣ dāgān*, apparently influenced by Deut 33:28; 2 Kgs 18:32; Isa 36:17.

[21]G has "fruit," perhaps in anticipation of its reading of *k^{e}gan rāwe(h)* as "like a fruit-bearing tree."

[22]The word *nepeš* is ambivalent, also having the connotation of "life force."

[23]G seems to presuppose **k^e'ēṣ p^{e}rî*, which must be an old variant.

[24]G erroneously reads this bicolon as *'āz *tiśmaḥnâ *b^{e}tûlôt *biqhal *baḥurîm ûz(^{e})qēnîm *yeḥ(ĕ)dû*.

[25]Not in G. Perhaps the MT conflates variants, since this colon is slightly overloaded. The state of the G in this section does not, however, instill confidence.

[26]G "I will make numerous and moisten" seems to reflect a conflation of the correct *w^{e}riwwêtî* and a corrupt **ribbîtî*, as *BHS* suggests.

[27]Instead of *dāšēn*, G reflects **b^{e}nê Lēwî*; MT is preferable.

[28]This seems to be a *topos* in Canaanite descriptions of military mobilization; cf. *CTA* 14.2.96-103; Isa 33:23-24; 35:5; 42:7,16; see Halpern, *The Constitution of the Monarchy in Israel* (HSM 25; Chico, California: Scholars Press, 1981) 318, n. 384.

[29]For the pastoral imagery, cf. Isa 40:11; 49:9; 63:11,14; Ezek 20:37; Ps 77:21; 78:52.

[30]Cf. Isa 11:16; 19:23; 35:8; 40:3; 43:19; 49:11; 62:10.

[31]Cf. Isa 51:3.

[32]G prefixes "therefore" as in vv 27,30. This may be original, in which case the MT has lost **lākēn* due to homoioteleuton with *wā'āben*.

[33]So (correctly) MT. G vocalizes **'ešpōṭ*, "so will I judge you."

[34]G has simply *kyrios*; perhaps this is the result of haplography in the Greek.

[35]G "my rod" is presumably explicative.

[36]Reading *w^{e}hēbē(')tî 'etkem *b^{e}mispār*, following G, though perhaps

the last word should be **bmsrt*, "by number"; on *msr*, "to count," see M. Greenberg, *Ezekiel 1-20* (AB 22; Garden City, New York: Doubleday, 1983) 373 or *idem*, "*MSRT HBRYT*, 'The obligation of the covenant,' in Ezekiel 20:27," *The Word of the Lord Shall Go Forth* (Fs. D. N. Freedman; Winona Lake, Indiana: Eisenbrauns, 1983) 37-46. MT *b^e māsōret habb^e rît* is viewed by most as a corruption of **b^e mispār* plus a garbled reduplication of the following *ûbārôtî*; see most recently Zimmerli, *Ezekiel* 1 (BKAT 13; Neukirchen: Neukirchener Verlag, 1969) 437. For the idiom, cf. 2 Chr 9:28. Greenberg (*MSRT HBRYT*) still defends the MT, but he is forced to create a new word *māsōret* < *ma(')sōret*, "obligation."

[37]G reads **kî* for *bî*.

[38]Reading, with G, **yābô'û* for MT *yābô(')*; *the wāw* was lost because of the initial *wāw* of the next word.

[39]G "remove" presumes a form of **'br*, probably the Piel imperative.

[40]This section seems garbled. The translation given here, while rather forced, is close to the MT; I assume that *l^e kû* is the equivalent of *l^e kû 'aḥărê* and repoint *w^e 'aḥar* as **'āḥēr*, taking the *wāw* to be dittographic. For other emendations, see Zimmerli, *Ezekiel* 1, 437. Greenberg (*Ezekiel*, 362,374) takes the MT at face value, translating, "Each of you go worship his idols, and afterwards, if you do not listen to me...," the unspoken apodosis being "I will give you your due." This rendering, however, creates the impression that Yahweh is telling Israel to go ahead and apostatize, if that is the only way for it to outgrow its idolatrous tendencies. I find this implausible.

[41]Lacking in G.

[42]Lacking in G. The problem is the similarity of *bā'āreṣ* and *'erṣēm* (or **'erṣe(h)*), exacerbated by the recurrence of *šām*, though it itself is not in doubt. Either the G reflects a haplography or the MT contains a dittography. The G reading is less redundant, but that is not certain grounds for a choice.

[43]G does not reflect any pronominal suffix and perhaps reads **'erṣe(h)*.

[44]Cf. Exod 6:6; Deut 4:34; 5:15; 7:19; 9:29; 11:2; 26:8 etc.

[45]Cf. Exod 33:11; Deut 34:10; also Num 12:8 ("mouth to mouth") and Gen 32:31, where the subject is Jacob.

[46]"Der 'neue Exodus' in der Verkündigung der beiden grossen Exilspropheten" (1960), *Gottes Offenbarung* (Theologische Bücherei 19; Munich: Kaiser, 1963) 194-197.

[47]*Theology of the Program of Restoration of Ezekiel* (HSM 10; Missoula, Montana: Scholars Press, 1976) 37-53.

[48]The MT *mittaḥat mikketep* is barely possible, but more likely we should read either *mittaḥat *ketep*, or, following G, simply

mikketep, assuming the *mittaḥat* to be a vertical dittography caused by the similarity of *yōṣᵉ'îm* and *yōrᵉdîm*.

[49]G does not translate *habbayit*.

[50]Or, "the north gate."

[51]So G; MT reflects a corruption of **hḥsr* to *ḥwṣ drk*, due to the similarity of *rêš* and *dālet* and under the influence of the preceding *derek ḥûṣ*.

[52]So MT; G "the water." Since the prior word ends in a *hē'*, haplography and dittography are both possible.

[53]Or perhaps "forward" with G.

[54]I.e., the line, which was a cubit in length. The man is measuring distance from the Temple.

[55]G "he passed," reading **wayya'ăbōr*. Similarly in v 4.

[56]*'Opsayim* is a *hapax legomenon*. The Vulgate, Peshitta and Targum translate "ankles." The G *aphesis*, "discharge," is simply an etymological speculation based upon the similarity of the Greek and Hebrew. *'Ōpes* may be a form of *'epes*, "extremity," but the connection of this word to the particle *'epes*, "only," the quasinoun "nothing" and Sumero-Akkadian *apsu* is obscure.

[57]We must read *mê* for MT *mayim*.

[58]Not in G.

[59]G "he." It is impossible to judge in vv 3-5 whether the man (G) or Ezekiel (MT) crosses the water.

[60]G *rhoizos*, "rushing," is indicative only of ignorance as to the meaning of the rare word *śāḥû*. We learn from this that Ezekiel (or perhaps the man) did not know how to swim.

[61]That the G renders *wayyôlīkēnî wayšībēnî* simply as *kai ēgagen me* may reflect loose translation or the loss of the second word due to homoioteleuton.

[62]See Zimmerli, *Ezekiel* 2, 1188.

[63]Or "forest."

[64]G incorrectly reads *mûṣā'îm* as a form of *yṣ'*, rather than *ṣw'*.

[65]So G, presupposing *'el-*hayyām *'el-*hammayim hammûṣā'îm*. MT has lost **'el-*hammayim* through homoioteleuton and added *hē'* to **hayyām* by dittography.

[66]So G. MT inexplicably has *naḥălayim*.

[67]Read **wᵉyērāpē'*, taking the *wāw* to be dittographic.

[68]For MT *wᵉhāyâ* (v 10), read **yihye(h)* with G.

[69]Read **yihye(h)* with G.

[70]G "its."

[71]*Biṣṣō(')tāw* is presumably the same as *biṣṣôtāw*.

[72]G *hyperarsis* erroneously derives *gebe'* from *gbh*, "to be high."

[73]G misreads *'ālēhû* as "upon him."

[74]G mistranslates *lḥdšyw* as "of its newest [fruit]."

75 The *k*^{e}*tīb w*^{e}*hāyû* is possible, but the *q*^{e}*rē w*^{e}*hāyâ* is stylistically preferable and supported by the G.

76 Here, too, the Greek translator is ignorant of the word *'āle(h)*, and this time he guesses *anabasis*, "rising."

77 See p. 11, 16, nn. 13-15.

78 Note that Ezekiel predicts that all the land will become like Eden in 36:35.

79 G here adds "Jerusalem," and translates the colon, "Awake, awake, O Jerusalem, don the strength of your arm," omitting *Yahwe(h)* at the end and rendering as though there were a suffix on *z*^{e}*rôa'*. This alteration is presumably due to the influence of Isa 51:17.

80 1QIsa[a] (M. Burrows, *The Dead Sea Scrolls of St. Mark's Monastery* 1 [New Haven, Connecticut: ASOR, 1950] pl. XLII) reads *hmwḥṣt*, as in Job 26:12, with identical meaning. Either is possible.

81 This bicolon has been lost in the G through homoioarchton with the following.

82 The ambiguity of *ḥrb* is probably intentional; at first one thinks it must refer to combat, but the following bicolon suggests drying.

83 MT perfect; read with G the participle (*inter alios* Dillmann, *Der Prophet Jesaia*[5] [Kurzgefasstes exegetisches Handbuch zum Alten Testament; Leipzig: Hirzel, 1890] 445-446).

84 Read with prior colon by G. 1QIsa[a] reads *pzwry*, which makes worse parallelism with *g*^{e}*'ûlîm* and is probably inauthentic.

85 Hebrew speaks of wearing emotions or other properties; cf. the first verse of this selection, or Ps 104:1. For the wearing of *śimḥâ*, cf. Ps 30:12. Note, too, that *p*^{e}*'ēr*, "glory," may also denote a head-dress.

86 Reading, with G, either **yaśśīgûm* or perhaps simply **yaśśīgû*, with *autous* having been added for clarity.

87 G "distress, pain and groaning" seems to represent a conflation of variant translations. Cf. 35:10.

88 This bicolon, which appears in almost the same form in Isa 35:10, may be treated in one of three ways. Above, I have followed the G in regarding *śāśôn, śimḥâ, yāgôn* and *'ănāḥâ* as subjects, rather than objects. This is easier if one emends to **yaśśīgûm*, but it is not absolutely necessary and is in any case more difficult for 35:10. One might object that it is bizarre to describe joy as "overtaking someone," but cf. Isa 59:10. The alternative is to see these emotions as objects and to translate "they will attain rejoicing and exultation; they will flee grief and groaning." The use of *nws* without a preposition is odd, but perhaps permissible in poetry; cf. *bā'û Ṣiyyôn* (51:11). Finally, one could solve the problem by sacrificing a measure of syntactic parallelism and rendering "they will attain rejoicing and exultation; grief and groaning will flee."

[89]Likewise extra-metrical. The subject of these imperatives is unclear. In the beginning of the verse it is obviously Israel, yet Israel is alluded to in the third person within the proclamation. This is not, of course, an insurmountable difficulty, as one may use the third person in speaking of oneself. F. M. Cross ("The Council of Yahweh in Second Isaiah," *JNES* 12 [1953] 277) believes that the addressees are the members of the divine assembly, while D. N. Freedman ("Structure") argues that in chaps. 34-35, 40-41 the subjects of the imperatives are the nations of the world; such could also be the case here.

[90]G "If they thirst."

[91]*Ḥŏrābôt* is a possible allusion to Horeb (Koenig, "Sourciers," 37, n. 1). G renders with a singular.

[92]G adds "and my people will drink," which is apparently borrowed from Exod 17:6. Note the *hysteron proteron* of this verse.

[93]Clifford (*Fair Spoken and Persuading* [New York: Paulist, 1984] 145) comments that the waters of the desert are a foretaste of the prosperity of 48:18; this is the aspect I will stress below.

[94]Reading as though from *nṣr*. G^{A} omits the word entirely, but other G MSS and patristic citations (see J. Ziegler, *Isaias*[3] [Göttingen Septuagint 14; Göttingen: Vandenhoeck & Ruprecht, 1983] 306) reflect a derivation from *yṣr*, "to form." Since the prior cola speak of victory, but this colon of creation of a covenant and a nation, either is possible, and ambiguity may be intentional. The verse is suspiciously prosaic, but it is unlikely to be corrupt, since the same words occur in 42:6.

[95]G "a covenant of nations." For a discussion of this peculiar expression, see M. Smith, "*Bĕrît 'Am/Bĕrît 'Ôlām*: A New Proposal for the Crux of Isaiah 42:6," *JBL* 100 (1981) 241-243.

[96]*Hēqîm* is peculiar, and the colon is too short. Perhaps the verse has suffered corruption and in the original *hēqîm* referred to *b^{e}rît* in some fashion. Clifford (*Fair Spoken*, 151), however, points out the correspondence with *l^{e}hāqîm 'et-šibṭê Ya'ăqōb*. Possibly the infinitives in vv 8-9 should be translated participially, referring to Yahweh.

[97]G presupposes *'al-*kol-d^{e}rākîm*, which could be an anticipation of the following colon, or could be original, having been lost in the Hebrew through homoioteleuton.

[98]G "roads" is apparently due to ignorance of the rare word *š^{e}pāyîm* (cf. G's desperate guesses in Num 23:3; Jer 3:2,21; 4:11; 7:29; 12:12; 14:6), though it is correctly rendered (for the sole time in the G) in Isa 41:18 as "mountains."

[99]So MT; G "every mountain," which may well be correct.

[100]G has here "and every road into their pasture." Apparently there

was a vertical dittography of *ûb(ᵉ)kol-šᵉpāyîm mar'îtām* from v 9 due to the presence of *derek* in both verses. Note that in v 9 *mar'ît* is translated *nomē* and here *boskēma*, proving that the error did not occur in the course of the Greek transmission of the G.

[101]Literally, "the sea."

[102]For MT *Sînîm* read **Sᵉwēnîm* with 1QIsa[a].

[103]Translating as an imperative with *qᵉrē*, 1QIsa[a] and G, rather than as a jussive with *kᵉtîb*. Either is possible.

[104]On the contacts of Jeremiah and Second Isaiah, see S. Paul, "Literary and Ideological Echoes of Jeremiah in Deutero-Isaiah," *World Congress of Jewish Studies, Fifth*, 1 (4 vols.; Jerusalem: World Union of Jewish Studies, 1969) 102-120.

[105]Here Second Isaiah plays upon our expectations. In the context of the Exodus, *hammôṣî'* ordinarily has as its object Israel; here it is the Egyptians.

[106]The precise interpretation of this colon is uncertain. To judge from Ps 24:8, *'izzûz* is a noun meaning "hero." On the other hand, *ḥayil* usually refers to an army. To maximize parallelism, we must suppose either that *ḥayil* here equals *'îš ḥayil, gibbôr ḥayil* etc., or else read the noun **'ězûz*, literally, "might." G renders "mighty multitude." Vs. MT, we must divide the cola after *yaḥdāw*.

[107]G has "like extinguished flax"; is this an interpretive translation, or did the *Vorlage* read **kōbâ*?

[108]G plural, no doubt under the influence of the prior verse.

[109]MT and G both have "rivers" (*nᵉhārôt*). This makes poor parallelism with "way," and is hence suspect. 1QIsa[a] reads *ntybwt*, "roads," which is probably correct. See J. C. Trever, "Isaiah 43:19 According to the First Isaiah Scroll (DSIa)," *BASOR* 121 (1951) 13-16. The received text has simply anticipated v 20.

[110]The G in v 16 skipped *bᵉyahwe(h)* due to homoioarchton, so that 16b was construed as a single colon. The final verb *tithallal* was then translated as if it were **yithallᵉlû*, referring to the "poor and the destitute" of v 17, yielding "the poor and destitute will exult; they will seek water...." While this cannot be correct, the authenticity of the MT is still questionable, since v 17a is overloaded. It seems, therefore, that we have a conflation of two variants (B. Duhm, *Das Buch Jesaia* [Göttinger Handkommentar zum Alten Testament 3.1; Göttingen: Vandenhoeck & Ruprecht, 1914] 280), of which *hā'ebyônîm* is perhaps to be preferred as the more unusual.

[111]G expands to *kyrios ho theos*.

[112]For MT *'ăgam-mayim* G reads **'ăgammîm*. The MT is preferable, since the prophet seems to be quoting Ps 114:8.

113It is preferable to break the colon after *'erez*, rather than after *šiṭṭâ*, as does the MT.

114The identity of these trees is uncertain; I have followed KB.

115G "all this" is expansionistic.

116The pronominal suffix is not reflected in the G.

117I accept the attribution of Isaiah 34-35 to Second Isaiah. See Pope, "Isaiah 34 in Relation to Isaiah 35, 40-66," *JBL* 71 (1952) 235-243 and the literature cited therein. See, too, Freedman, "Structure."

118G reads, without the conjunction, "the parched desert."

119Reading either **yāśīśû*, taking the final *mēm* to be dittographic, or, supposing *nûn-mēm* interchange, **yeśīśûn*, though it is conceivable that Second Isaiah employs the enclitic *mēm* as an affectation.

120To be read with v 2, vs. MT. Perhaps we should emend to **baḥabăṣṣelet* or **baḥabăṣṣālōt*, "with *ḥabaṣṣelet*-flower(s)."

121MT *'ap gîlat werannēn* is probably corrupt; the simplest restoration is *'ap* **gîl* **terannēn*, "let it sing out (in) joy"; one might also read an infinite absolute **gôl* (Cross, orally). G's "the deserts of the Jordan" is probably based upon a misreading or a corruption.

122G has the conjunction.

123"Sharon" not in G.

124G reflects **'ammî* for MT *hēmmâ*, but perhaps this is simply interpretive. In the MT, however, it seems that *hēmmâ* refers to the mountains, not to Israel. Alternatively, it is conceivable that we have a form analogous to Ugaritic *hm*, "behold" (Cross, orally).

125G reflects **'ĕlōhîm*; Cross (*Canaanite Myth*, 171) restores **'ĕlōhê 'ôlām*.

126G reads **ḥizqû*, "be strong," but the proper form would be **ḥăzaqnâ*, so the hands themselves are probably not the addressees. Based on the parallel with Ezra 6:22, it is most likely that, as Freedman suggests, the nations are commanded to encourage the Israelites.

127*'Imrû* is omitted in the G due to homoioteleuton and overall graphic similarity to *'ammeṣû*, which the G reads with v 4 as **'ĭmṣû*, translating "take heart, O [vocative *lāmed*] fainthearted."

128G "our" is more likely to be an inner-Greek corruption from *hymōn* to *hēmōn* than a reflection of a variant *Vorlage*.

129Reading **nōqēm* for MT *nāqām* enables us to divide the cola in this fashion, yielding superior symmetry.

130G translates this colon, "Behold, our [for "your"] god requites and will requite in judgment." Presumably, this reflects **hinnē(h) 'ĕlōhêkem nōqēm* [*sic!*] *yiqqōm gemûl*, with an infinitive absolute *nqm* misread as a participle. **Yiqqōm* replaces MT *yābô(')*, and *'ělōhîm* is not translated. If this is the original text, the MT has suffered an upwards vertical dittography of the first *yābô(')* and a downwards dittography of *'ělōhîm*. The resultant text, however, is excessively prosaic; it is better to see the G's **nqm yqm* as a horizontal dittography and the loss of *'ělōhîm* as an error. Cross orally suggests a reading *hinnē(h) 'ělōhêkem nāqām/* yābî' g*[e]*mûl 'ělōhîm*, with *nāqām* and *g*[e]*mûl* being both the objects of *yābî'*.

131 Reading **w*[e]*yôšî'ăkem*. P. Wernberg-Møller ("Two Difficult Passages in the Old Testament," *ZAW* 69 (1957) 71-73 solves the problem of this verse in a different fashion by, rather implausibly, interpreting *'ělōhêkem* as an alloform of *'ălêkem* and by more plausibly reading the last word as *w*[e]*yiš'ăkem* with Ehrlich, *Randglossen* 4, 126. This yields the translation "Behold, to you vengeance will come, the recompense of God will come, and (so will) your salvation." We may accept the second reading without the first, translating, "Behold your god avenges; the retribution of God comes; it comes (along with) your victory."

132 G "will hear" probably does not reflect a variant *Vorlage*, but rather the effort to avoid repeating "will be opened" used to translate *tippāqaḥnâ* in the prior colon.

133 G *tranē estai*, "will be distinct," is a wordplay with Hebrew *tārōn*; see C. P. Caspari, "Jesaja 34 und 35," *ZAW* 49 (1931) 77, n. 1.

134 G singular.

135 G reads **'ăgammîm*, itself conceivably a corruption of **'ăgam-mayim*. I take the MT to be original and the G to reflect an assimilation to v 7a and v 7c, both of which end in *mayim*.

136 G singular.

137 G translates "pleasure," as though from *n'y*, yet correctly translates *epaulis* in Isa 34:13.

138 G unaccountably translates *tannîm* as "birds."

139 MT *ribṣāh*, "her pasture," cannot be correct; even if we read with Rashi and some Hebrew MSS **ribṣâ*, "a pasture," the imagery is inconsistent. G omits the word altogether, or else has combined it with *tannîm* and interpreted the result as the name of a bird. 1QIsa[a] has *rbṣ*, apparently also "pasture."

Isa 35:7 must be read in conjunction with 34:13, where the fertile land becomes a barren desert covered with scrub. In 35:7 the process is reversed. The land turns from a desert, the abode of jackals, into a luxuriant swamp. The context requires in v 7c a word referring to water. One solution is to delete the *rêš* and read **biṣṣâ*. Note that this word is used in Job 8:11 and 40:21 in conjunction with *gōme'* and *qāne(h)*. Moreover, the addition of the *rêš* is fairly easy to account for, since the word *nāwe(h)/nā'e(h)* often occurs in association with the root *rbṣ* (Isa 27:10; 65:10; Jer

33:12; Ezek 25:5; 34:14; Zeph 2:6-7; Ps 23:2; Prov 24:15). J. Blau ("Marginalia Semitica 1," *Israel Oriental Studies 1* [1971] 10-11), however, points out the association of the root *rbṣ* in Hebrew and Aramaic with irrigation and plausibly deduces that **ribṣâ* is a *hapax legomenon* meaning "irrigation."

140 Blau ("Marginalia," 8-9) shows that here grass is a symbol of desolation. His similar interpretation of the MT of Isa 34:13 is persuasive: "And it will be an abode of jackals, and grass (suitable) for (the pasture of) ostriches (?) (will be there)."

141 G seems to read *maslûl* **ṭāhôr*, and 1QIsa^{a} skips the first *wdrk* altogether, presumably through haplography.

142 Instead of MT *w*^{e}*hāyâ*, 1QIsa^{a} reads *yhyh*.

143 Perhaps read **lōh* for MT *lāh*, as suggested by *BHS*, but see n. 145.

144 This is the reconstruction, orally conveyed, of Cross; the Hebrew is *lō(') ya'abrennû ṭāmē' w*^{e}*hāl*^{e}*kû g*^{e}*'ûlîm bô/derek ûp(*^{e}*)zûrîm lō(') yit'û*; cf. similar treatment in *Canaanite Myth*, 172, n. 116. Cross is probably correct that both *we'ĕwîlîm* and *w*^{e}*hû' lāmô* are corruptions of *(hag)g*^{e}*'ûlîm*.

145 MT *ya'ălennâ* has a feminine suffix; contrast *ya'abrennû* in v 8 and compare MT *lāh* in v 8. Apparently the author could not decide whether he was speaking of a *maslûl* (masculine) or a *derek* (feminine); perhaps, therefore, we should not re-point *lh* in v 8.

146 Either something is missing here or a variant has been incorporated into the text. Cross (*Canaanite Myth*, 172, n. 117) reconstructs "no lion will be found there; no beast of prey will mount it," taking *lō(') yihye(h) šammâ* to be intrusive.

147 Restoring with Duhm (*Jesaia*, 231) *w*^{e}*hāl*^{e}*kû* **bô*, lost by homoioteleuton, on the basis of the G, though this is not absolutely necessary.

148 On the problems of v 10, see above, p. 115, n. 88.

149 Cf. Isa 11:6-8; the description of Dilmun in "Enki and Ninhursag" and the relation of Enkidu with the beasts in the Epic of Gilgamesh.

150 Cf. Isa 29:17-18, which alludes to Carmel, Lebanon and the healing of the deaf and blind.

151 I omit from this discussion Isa 58:11, part of so-called Third Isaiah, though by the conventional translation it contains another allusion to Water in the Wilderness. The crux is *ṣaḥṣāḥôt*, ordinarily translated "desert(s)." In light of the word order and the G rendering "you will be sated according to the desire of your soul," I think we must seek a different translation. I follow D. Qimḥi (*Miqrā'ôt G*^{e}*dôlôt* 7 [Jerusalem: Pardes, 1954] 83b) in understanding *ṣaḥṣāḥôt* (or **ṣaḥṣāḥût*) as "parchedness," translating the entire verse, "he soothes your parched throat." For the related

root *ṣḥy* used of thirst, cf. Isa 5:13.

152 G has the variant "my son,"

153 One could read either a participle (with the MT and G) or revocalize to **'ās^{e}kā*, which is a better parallel to *ya'z^{e}rekkā*, inasmuch as both are finite verbs.

154 G translates "you will yet be helped" and connects it to the following, but this seems to be a makeshift treatment of a poorly understood passage.

155 Here, too, G has "son."

156 G has "beloved Israel." *Agapēmenos* is a common rendering of *Y^{e}šūrûn*; it seems that the translator has conflated 44:1b and 2d.

157 G unaccountably has "upon those who wander in the desert."

158 In v 3 "as...so" are not in the MT, but are implied by the coordination; cf. 55:10-11, where *kî ka'ăšer...kēn* is explicit. Note that 1QIs^{a} actually contains a interlinear gloss *kn*.

159 Reading the preposition **k^{e}-* for MT *b^{e}-*, following G, 1QIsa^{a} and Targum.

160 See Allegro, "The Meaning of *BYN* in Isaiah XLIV, 4," *ZAW* 63 (1951) 154-156. Allegro reads for *ḥāṣîr* **ḥāṣôr*, a hypothetical word for "green." For the metaphor, cf. Jer 17:8; Ps 1:3; 92:13-15. G "like grass in the midst of water" seems to be a conjecture.

161 G "rejoice" is based on a reading of either **hārî'û* or *harnînû*.

162 G imperative, presumably to heighten parallelism.

163 Read **tippātaḥ* with Syriac, Targum and Vulgate.

164 Reading either **w^{e}yīper* or, with 1QIsa^{a}, **w^{e}yipraḥ*. For this colon G has "let the earth sprout mercy," apparently reflecting a variant **tipraḥ hā'āreṣ ḥesed* (?). Perhaps we should read **w^{e}yaprû*, with *šāmayim* and/or *š^{e}ḥāqîm* as the subject. The verse is awkward and may well contain conflated variants.

165 Instead of MT *taṣmîaḥ*, we should read either **taṣmaḥ* (jussive, with G) or **tiṣmaḥ* without substantially altering the sense. In any case, the verbs that go with *yešaʿ* and *ṣ^{e}dāqâ* should be of the same conjugation, whether Qal or Hiphil.

166 This passage, which concludes the prophecy of Second Isaiah (or at least his oracles delivered in Exile, if we attribute to him all of Isaiah 34-35, 40-66), seems not to be poetic, despite a certain amount of parallelism. It is better described as rhetorical.

167 Not reflected in G; perhaps it dropped from the Greek due to homoioteleuton.

168 G seems to read **'aṣlîaḥ* and to insert **dark^{e}kā*.

169 1QIsa^{a} reads the more common *tēl^{e}kû* for the MT *tûbālûn*; cf. Syriac.

170 G has the conjunction at the beginning of the verse.

171 One could regard this as a lifting of the curse of Gen 3:17-19. It may

be that J, at least, considered the curse removed in Gen 8:21, but more likely the curse there refers to the Flood.

[172] See Clifford, *Fair Spoken.*

[173] See Y. Kaufmann, *The Babylonian Captivity and Deutero-Isaiah* (*History of the Religion of Israel* 4; Hebrew Original 1937-1956; New York: Union of American Hebrew Congregations, 1970) 7-9; on the fifth century see M. D. Coogan, "Life in the Diaspora," *BA* 37 (1974) 6-12.

[174] Cf. Ezra 8:22.

[175] On the archeology and history of this period, see E. Janssen, *Juda in der Exilszeit* (Forschungen zur Religion und Literatur des Alten und Neuen Testaments: Göttingen: Vandenhoeck & Ruprecht, 1956); P. Ackroyd, *Exile and Restoration* (OTL; Philadelphia, Pennsylvania: Westminster, 1968) 20-38; S. Weinberg, "*'Ereṣ-Yiśrā'ēl 'aḥărê ḥorban bayit rī(')šôn,*" *Proceedings of the Israel Academy of Science and Humanities* 4 (Jerusalem: Israel Academy of Science and Humanities, 1971) 202-216.

[176] See R. Rendtorff, "Die theologische Stellung des Schöpfungsglaubens bei Deuterojesaja," *ZTK* 51 (1954) 3-13; C. Stuhlmueller, "The Theology of Creation in Second Isaias," *CBQ* 21 (1959) 429-467; P. B. Harner, "Creation Faith in Deutero-Isaiah," *VT* 17 (1967) 298-306.

[177] See Cross, *Canaanite Myth*, 136-144.

[178] G "For I now will comfort you, Zion" is probably periphrastic. It may be, however, that the tense is correct; in poetry the use of the verbal aspects is fluid, and the first verb, at least, could be lightly emended to **y^{e}naḥēm*, if one wished for a true imperfect.

[179] MT *wayyāśem*, "he made," is probably to be read **w^{e}yāśīm*, "he will make," in conformity both to the situation of the prophet and to the G's "I will make."

[180] G runs together these two cola, skipping from one *k^{e}*- to the other and translating "And I will make her desert like the garden of the Lord." For the sentiment, compare Ezek 36:35.

[181] G reads **yimṣ^{e}'û*, "they will find," but the MT is preferable, since the G is perhaps paraphrasing.

[182] Pp. 33-34.

[183] Beyerlin has devoted an entire monograph (*Werden und Wesen des 107. Psalms* [BZAW 153; Berlin: De Gruyter, 1978]) to this text; I can comment only briefly here upon his views. In essence, he believes that the original, post-exilic psalm consisted of vv 1, 4-22, and that it referred not to the return from exile, but to Yahweh's aid to persons in distress, presented stereotypically as wanderers in the desert (vv 4-9), prisoners (vv 10-16) and invalids (vv 17-22, as interpreted by Beyerlin, 48-49). The psalm ended with a call to

sacrifice. To this was added yet another type of distress, that of sailors at sea (vv 23-32). Next, vv 2-3 were inserted; only now was the distress of vv 4-32 taken as a reference to the exile. Finally, vv 33-43 were added as a new conclusion. Beyerlin is led to this analysis by his keen perception of shifting interests throughout the psalm, in particular his detection of Wisdom motifs. He shows convincingly that the sufferings of vv 4-32 are presented as stereotypical and maintains that since reference to exile is so assiduously avoided, they cannot be of the same authorship as vv 2-3. I, however, am dubious of theories of accretion and would rather see one author playing with our expectations and mixing genres in order to give a sapiential interpretation of Israel's return. Once it is realized that Psalms 105-107 constitute a unit, it is clear that Psalm 107 speaks of return from exile. Note that the thematic and verbal contacts among the three psalms (see above, p. 34) cut across all of Beyerlin's putative layers of Psalm 107. We must, however, take seriously Beyerlin's emphasis upon the sapiential cast. Its role in the entire triptych requires further study; notice, for instance, the proverbial form of Ps 106:3.

184 It seems that all three psalms originally began *hall^e lû-yâ*, as in the G. The MT has transferred this phrase from the beginning of Psalms 105 and 107 to the end of the prior psalm, while it is repeated at the end of Psalm 105 and the beginning of 106.

185 It may be possible to take *kî*, not as the conjunction, but as introducing indirect discourse after the verb of speech *hôdû*. The ambivalence of *kî* is clear if we compare Ps 118:1-4, where *hôdû...kî* parallels *yō(')mar/yō(')m^e rû...kî*, and Psalm 136, where the only possible renderings of *kî* are "for" or perhaps "indeed."

186 Beyerlin (*107. Psalm*, 25) takes *'ăšer* to be synonymous to *kî* and a sign of lateness, yet it is more natural to read it as the relative pronoun.

187 Deleting the conjunction with G.

188 G has "and from."

189 Both MT and G have "from north and the sea," i.e., west. The Targum has *d^e rōmā'* (i.e. **yāmîn*), but this is hardly likely to be based upon a variant text. Note that a sea voyage is depicted in vv 23-30. Beyerlin (pp. 22-23) argues the dependence of these verses upon Isa 43:5-6 and 49:12. Other biblical parallels are Deut 30:3-5; Isa 11:12; 40:11; 49:18,22; 56:8; Jer 23:3; 29:14; 31:8,10; 32:37; Ezek 11:17; 20:34,41; 34:13; 36:24; 37:21; 39:27; Zeph 3:19,20; Zech 2:10; 10:8-10; Ps 106:47=1 Chr 16:35.

190 Reading, as suggested by *BHS*, **tō'ê* for *tā'û* to enhance parallelism with vv 10, 23.

191 Divide the cola here with G, vs. MT.

[192]G has the conjunction.

[193]G has the plural here and in vv 15 and 31; i.e., *ḥăsādāw for MT ḥasdô. This is possible, and in fact it heightens the parallelism with *nipl^{e}'ôtāw*. Beyerlin (p. 75) stresses, however, the allusion to *hasdo* of v 1, so we should most likely follow the MT. Syriac reads *ḥăsīdāw, which, though it reflects a correct understanding of the addressees as the redeemed of v 2, is unlikely. By the time this psalm was written, *ḥsd* and *ḥsyd* were always distinguished; the Syriac translator, however, accustomed to defective spellings in older parts of the Bible and ignorant of the history of Hebrew orthography, might naturally have assumed *ḥsdw* to be ambiguous. Since scribal transmission introduced some defective spelling into all sections of the Bible, however, this argument alone is insufficient grounds for completely dismissing the reading *ḥăsīdāw. A greater problem is that it destroys the parallelism.

[194]This translation, proffered by Dahood [*Psalms* 3, 83], is the best that has been proposed.

[195]Presumably, v 9a refers to liquid and v 9b to solid refreshment.

[196]This bicolon quotes almost *verbatim* Isa 41:18 and echoes 42:15; 44:27; 50:2.

[197]Here the MT begins to use converted imperfects, but we may well doubt if this is correct.

[198]See Beyerlin, *107. Psalm*, 13-31.

SUMMARY AND CONCLUSIONS

The foregoing chapters have traced the varied manifestations of the Water in the Wilderness motif. As the resonances of the motif are clearest in the latest texts, we will review our findings in reverse, which may clarify certain points. For schematic purposes, we may identify three levels of association for the Water in the Wilderness motif: 1)the mythic, referring to Creation; 2)the historical, referring to the desert wandering following the Exodus; 3)the contemporary, referring to the time of the text. At level 1 the entire world is irrigated; at level 2 the people are given drink; at level 3 Canaan is fertilized. Level 2, like level 1, describes formative events and may follow mythic patterns.

Chapter Four: Building upon the Hosean and Jeremianic predictions of a recapitulation of the events of Moses' day, Ezekiel and Second Isaiah prophesy a new march through the desert, now the Syrian desert separating Babylon and Judah. Ezekiel focuses on the Sinai/Horeb tradition, depicting Mount Zion as the site of a new lawgiving and the source of healing waters, but Second Isaiah stresses instead the miracle of the water itself, irrespective of its origin. Both writers see the fructification of the barren land as a parallel to the events of creation as well as a promise of renewed fertility in Canaan. In other words, they employ all three levels of association.

Chapter Three: One might have assumed that the synthesis of the mythological, historical and contemporary associations of the Water in the Wilderness motif is a development of the Exile, but in fact it pervades Israelite literature from all periods. Even the tradition of the rebellion at Massah and Meribah, which operates primarily at level 2, is used as a parallel to primordial or contemporary events. Like Ezekiel, the Elohist regards Yahweh's mountain as the source of waters, an image rooted in the world of biblical and pre-biblical myth (level 1). At the same time, the rebellion traditions are not preserved out of merely antiquarian curiosity (level 2), but rather they advise the Israelites of the dangers of disobedience and the rewards of fidelity (level 3). Other texts omit the first level in referring to the rebellion at

Massah and Meribah: Psalm 81 cites the rebellion tradition to show that the Israelites have a clear choice between obedience and fertility, on the one hand, and rebellion and alienation, on the other (levels 2 and 3). Psalm 95 also operates at levels 2 and 3, but concentrates exclusively upon obedience and rebellion, ignoring any rewards or punishments. The versions of Massah-Meribah found in Deuteronomy 33 and Numbers 20 also function at levels 2 and 3, inasmuch as they reflect later competing claims to the priesthood, but they do not refer to fertility.

Chapter Two: Psalm 78, Deuteronomy 8-11 and Psalms 105-7, which speak simply of water in the desert, make little or no reference to Creation (level 1), but do contain morals for their audience as well as historical information (levels 3 and 2). Psalm 114 and Deuteronomy 32, on the other hand, seem to have all three associations, alluding to Creation, the desert period, and the fertility of Canaan.

Chapter One: We began with a brief discussion of the Ugaritic Epic of Ba'lu, though the field could easily have been expanded to include myths of Dumuzi, Osiris and Telepinus, not to mention non-Near Eastern sources, which likewise seek to account for the co-existence of fertility and sterility. Life[1] and Death are viewed as amoral personalities who fight under the compulsion of their very natures. Though human existence hangs in the balance at their encounter, these gods show little concern for humanity, but great care for their prestige. While these myths assign humanity a lowly place in the Cosmos, they console their audience with the implication that at least the interchange of life and death is predictable, its pattern having been established in primordial days. But the overall mood such myths convey to us today is resignation—resignation to Man's role in the world and resignation to the reign of Death.

Israel also sought an explanation for the existence of sterility and death beside fertility, but only allowed for the existence of one god "who fashions light and creates dark, makes prosperity and creates adversity" (Isa 45:7). Moreover, unlike the older Near Eastern civilizations, the Israelites put Man at the pinnacle of creation. With the greater glory came greater responsibility, for Yahweh would dispense either life or death *to the world* according to the merit of humanity. According to J, the world had been created a deathless paradise and would still be one, were it not for human disobedience, and Yahweh once nearly destroyed all his work in a flood because of the wickedness of Man. In other words, sterility was not inevitable, and even human death had not been part of Yahweh's original plan for the world, but both were brought about by sin.

The pattern of the Eden story, rebellion in the midst of fertility, followed by punishment, recurs throughout the Bible. But the Bible contracts its field of interest in its first twelve chapters into the figure of Abraham, i.e., Israel, and, because of the Bible's limited interest, the pattern plays itself out principally in the arena of Canaan. As Adam and Eve are expelled from Fertility (*'Ēden*) for their sin, so the Canaanites and Israelites are expelled from Canaan, or else the land's fertility is removed, which comes to the same thing. We are no longer in the world of mythology, where contemporary events follow a pattern built into the universe. On the contrary, the biblical stories of the Fall and of rebellion in the desert set a pattern of conditionality. Though conditionality is itself in theory predictable, since the covenant obliges Yahweh to reward fidelity, in fact it is so flexible that almost any calamity can be attributed to the guilt of the Israelites. The biblical picture of a god dispensing or withholding fertility according to ethical judgment is terrifying compared with the mythic conception that optimistically regards periodic fertility as structured into the universe.[2]

Israel's historical tradition was shaped partly by real events, partly by contemporary politics (e.g., priestly or regional rivalries) and partly by literary efforts to enhance its beauty, interest and moral value. Perhaps unconsciously, the Israelites adapted their historical memories to the patterns of myth, and it is quite possible that cultic factors abetted this process, since the major festivals, which celebrated both historical events and the natural cycle, probably had roots in Canaanite religion.[3] To phrase it simply, the agricultural festivals commemorated the triumph of fertility over sterility *in time*, in the passage of the seasons, while the historical tradition commemorated the alternation of sterility and fertility *in space*, in the journeys of Israel from Egypt, via the desert, to the mountain spring in the desert or to Canaan.[4] The power of providing water in the desert demonstrated, *a fortiori*,

Yahweh's power to irrigate his own land.

We can carry our analysis a step further by connecting the Water in the Wilderness tradition to the Exodus tradition, since both are rooted in Canaanite myth. The Ugaritic Epic of Ba'lu falls into two parts—1)a conquest of the Sea and the establishment of kingship over the world and 2)a victory (if only temporary) over Death and the establishment of fertility. The sequence is natural; once Ba'lu has driven back the waters to claim the dry land, he must fertilize it, or at least establish a *modus vivendi* with the conflicting power of sterility. The same sequence of events may be detected in Israelite tradition. Yahweh conquers the sea and establishes kingship over Israel; he conquers the barren desert by giving water to the people. That is, the role of Israel is the role of the Earth itself in Canaanite myth, and its arrival at the flowing mountain of Yahweh, whether Horeb, Canaan, Zion or anonymous, corresponds to the moment of the resurrection of Ba'lu, when the "the heavens rain oil; the wadis run with honey."

[1]In the person of a water-giving god. On water as the symbol *par excellence* of life, see Reymond, *L'eau*, 1-8 and *passim.*

[2]The fearsome aspect of the transition from archetypical to historical thought is stressed by Eliade, *Eternal Return.* On Israelite and Near Eastern attitudes towards fertility and sterility see J. Pedersen, *Israel: Its Life and Culture I-II* (2 vols.; Danish original 1920; London: Oxford, 1926) 204-212, 453-463, A. Haldar, *The Notion of the Desert in Sumero-Akkadian and West-Semitic Religions* (Uppsala Universitets Årsskrift 1950:3; Uppsala: Almqvist & Wiksell, 1950), R. Patai, "The 'Control of Rain' in Ancient Palestine," *HUCA* 14 (1939) 251-286 and Watson, *Mot,* 222-286.

[3]Cross, too (*Canaanite Myth* 79-111), sees ritual as a medium of the transfer of literary patterns and motifs from Canaanite myth to Israelite historiography.

[4]Theoretically, the mythological analogue to this in Canaanite myth would be the partitioning of the deserts to Môtu, while Ba'lu would rule the inhabitable regions. On the association of the desert with Death see N. J. Tromp (*Primitive Conceptions of Death and the Nether World in the Old Testament* [Biblica et Orientalia 21; Rome: PBI, 1969] 53, 131-132), P. A. Riemann ("Desert and Return to Desert in the Pre-exilic Prophets" [Harvard diss., 1964] 60-139) and Watson ("Mot," 146-147, 172-174).

BIBLIOGRAPHY

Aberbach, M., and Smolar, L., "Aaron, Jeroboam, and the Golden Calves," *JBL* 86 (1967) 129-140.

Abou-Assaf, A., Bordreuil, P., and Millard, A. R., *La statue de Tell Fekheryeh* (Études Assyriologiques 7; Paris: Recherche sur les civilisations, 1982).

Ackroyd, P., *Exile and Restoration* (OTL; Philadelphia, Pennsylvania: Westminster, 1968).

Albright, W. F., "The Babylonian Matter in the Predeuteronomic Primeval History (JE) in Gen 1-11," *JBL* 58 (1939) 91-103.

_____"The Mouth of the Rivers," *AJSLL* 35 (1919) 161-195.

_____"The Old Testament and Canaanite Language and Literature," *CBQ* 7 (1945) 5-31.

_____"Some Remarks on the Song of Moses in Deuteronomy XXXII," *VT* 9 (1959) 339-346.

Allegro, J. M., "Further Messianic References in Qumran Literature," *JBL* 75 (1956) 174-187.

_____"The Meaning of *BYN* in Isaiah XLIV, 4," *ZAW* 63 (1951) 154-156.

_____, ed., *Qumran Cave 4 I (4Q158-4Q186)* (DJD 5; Oxford: Clarendon, 1968).

Auerbach, E., *Moses* (German original 1953; Detroit, Michigan: Wayne State, 1975).

Avishur, Y., "The Ghost-expelling Incantation from Ugarit (Ras Ibn Ḥani 78/20)," *UF* 13 (1981) 13-25

Baillet, M., Milik, J. T., and de Vaux, R., *Les 'petites grottes' de Qumrân* (2 vols.; DJD 3; Oxford: Clarendon, 1962).

Barnes, W. E., *The Psalms* (2 vols.; Westminster Commentaries; London: Methuen, 1931).

Barrelet, M.-T., "Une peinture de la cour 106 du palais de Mari," *Studia Mariana* (ed. A. Parrot; Leiden: Brill, 1950).

Bauer, T., "Ein viertes altbabylonisches Fragment des Gilgameš-Epos," *JNES* 16 (1957) 254-262.

Beegle, D. M., *Moses, the Servant of Yahweh* (Grand Rapids, Michigan: Eerdmans, 1972).

Beyerlin, W., *Herkunft und Geschichte des ältesten Sinaitraditionen* (Tübingen: Mohr [Siebeck], 1961).

_____ *Werden und Wesen des 107. Psalms* (BZAW 153; Berlin: De Gruyter, 1978).

Biename', G., *Moïse et le don de l'eau dans la tradition juive ancienne: targum et midrash* (AnBib 98; Rome: PBI, 1984).

Blachère, R., Chouémi, M., and Denizeau, C., *Dictionnaire Arabe-Français-Anglais* (Paris: Maisonneuve et Larose, 1967-).

Blau, J., "Marginalia Semitica I," *Israel Oriental Studies* 1 (1971) 1-35.

_____ "On Problems of Polyphony and Archaism in Ugaritic Spelling," *JAOS* 88 (1968) 523-526.

Borger, R., *Babylonisch-akkadische Lesestücke* (3 vols.; Rome: PBI, 1963).

Brekelmans, C., "Die sogenannten deuteronomischen Elemente in Genesis bis Numeri," *Volume du congrès, Genève, 1965* (VTSup 15; Leiden: Brill, 1966) 90-96.

Briggs, C. A., and Briggs, E. G., *A Critical and Exegetical Commentary on the Book of Psalms* (2 vols.; ICC; Edinburgh: Clark, 1906).

Buchanan, B. *Catalogue of Ancient Near Eastern Seals in the Ashmolean Museum* (2 vols.; Oxford, Clarendon, 1962).

Budd, P. J., *Numbers* (Word Bible Commentary 5; Waco, Texas: Word, 1984).

Buis, P., "Qadesh, un lieu maudit," *VT* 24 (1974) 268-285.

Burney, C. F., *The Book of Judges* (first published separately in 1918) *and Notes on the Hebrew Text of the Books of Kings* (1903) (New York: KTAV, 1970).

Burrows, M., *The Dead Sea Scrolls of St. Mark's Monastery* 1 (New Haven, Connecticut: ASOR, 1950).

Campbell, A. F., "Psalm 78: A Contribution to the Theology of Tenth Century Israel," *CBQ* 41 (1979) 51-79.

Caquot, A., "*D^e^baš*," *TWAT* 2. 135-139.

Carlson, R. A., "Élie à l'Horeb," *VT* 19 (1969) 416-439.

Carroll, R. P., "The Elijah-Elisha Sagas: Some Remarks on Prophetic Succession in Ancient Israel," *VT* 19 (1969) 400-415.

Caspari, C. P., "Jesaja 34 und 35," *ZAW* 49 (1931) 67-86.

Cassuto, U., A Commentary on the Book of Exodus (Hebrew original 1944 ; Jerusalem: Magnes, 1967).

_____ *A Commentary on the Book of Genesis* (2 vols.; Hebrew original 1944; Jerusalem: Magnes, 1961).

_____"Deuteronomy Chapter XXXIII and the New Year in Ancient Israel" (1928), *Biblical and Oriental Studies* 1 (Jerusalem: Magnes, 1973) 47-70.

Childs, B. S., *The Book of Exodus* (OTL; Philadelphia, Pennsylvania: Westminster, 1974).

Clements, R. E., *Exodus* (Cambridge Bible Commentary; Cambridge: University, 1972).

Clifford, R. J., *The Cosmic Mountain in Canaan and the Old Testament* (HSM 4; Cambridge, Massachusetts: Harvard, 1972).

_____ *Fair Spoken and Persuading* (New York: Paulist, 1984).

_____"In Zion and David a New Beginning: An Interpretation of Psalm 78," *Traditions in Transformation* (Fs. F. M. Cross; eds. B. Halpern and J. D. Levenson; Winona Lake, Indiana: Eisenbrauns, 1981) 121-141.

_____"Style and Purpose in Psalm 105," *Bib* 60 (1979) 420-427.

Coats, G. W., *Rebellion in the Wilderness* (Nashville: Abingdon, 1968).

Coogan, M. D., "Life in the Diaspora," *BA* 37 (1974) 6-12.

Cornill, C. H., "Beiträge zur Pentateuchkritik," *ZAW* 11 (1891) 1-34.

Crenshaw, J. L., "*Wĕdōrēk ʿal-bāmŏtê ʾāreṣ,*" *CBQ* 34 (1972) 39-53.

Cross, F. M., *Canaanite Myth and Hebrew Epic* (Cambridge, Massachusetts: Harvard, 1973).

_____"The Development of the Jewish Scripts," *The Bible and the Ancient Near East* (Fs. W. F. Albright; ed. G. E. Wright; Garden City, New York: Doubleday, 1961) 133-202.

_____"The Epic Traditions of Early Israel: Epic Narrative and the Reconstruction of Early Israel," *The Poet and the Historian* (ed. R. E. Friedman; Harvard Semitic Studies; Chico, California: Scholars Press, 1983) 13-39.

Cross, F. M., Jr., and Freedman, D. N., *Studies in Ancient Yahwistic Poetry* (SBL Dissertation 21; Hopkins diss., 1950; Missoula, Montana: Scholars Press, 1975).

Dahood, M., "Eblaite *ì-du* and Hebrew *'ēd*, 'Rain Cloud'," *CBQ* 43 (1981) 534-537.

_____ "Philological Notes on the Psalms," *TS* 14 (1953) 85-88.

_____ *Psalms* (AB 16-17a; Garden City, New York: Doubleday, 1965-1970).

_____ "Zacharia 9,1, *'Ên 'Ādām*," *CBQ* 25 (1963) 123-124.

Davies, G. H., "Psalm 95," *ZAW* 85 (1973) 183-195.

Delitzsch, F., *Biblischer Commentar über die Psalmen* (Leipzig: Dörffling und Franke, 1873).

Dhorme, P., "L'arbre de vérité et l'arbre de vie," *RB* 4 (1907) 271-274.

Dillmann, A., *Die Genesis*[3] (Kurzgefasstes exegetisches Handbuch zum Alten Testament; Leipzig: Hirzel, 1892).

_____ *Numeri, Deuteronomium und Josua*[5] (Kurzgefasstes exegetisches Handbuch zum Alten Testament; Leipzig: Hirzel, 1886).

_____ *Der Prophet Jesaia*[5] (Kurzgefasstes exegetisches Handbuch zum Alten Testament; Leipzig: Hirzel, 1890).

Driver, G. R., "Once Again: Birds in the Bible," *PEQ* 90 (1958) 56-58.

Driver, S. R., *The Book of Exodus* (Cambridge Bible for Schools and Colleges; Cambridge: University, 1911).

_____ *An Introduction to the Literature of the Old Testament*[2] (Edinburgh: Clark, 1891).

Duhm, B., *Das Buch Jesaia* (Göttinger Handkommentar zum Alten Testament 3.1; Göttingen: Vandenhoeck & Ruprecht, 1914).

Dummermuth, F., "Zur deuteronomistischen Kulttheologie und ihren Voraussetzungen," *ZAW* 70 (1958) 59-98.

Dussaud, R., *Les origins canaanéenes du sacrifice israelite*[2] (Paris: Presses Universitaires de France, 1941).

Eaton, J. H., "Some Questions of Philology and Exegesis in the Psalms," *JTS* 19 (1968) 603-609.

Ehrlich, A. B., *Randglossen zur hebräischen Bibel* (7 vols.; Leipzig: Hinrich, 1909).

Eissfeldt, O., "Die älteste Erzählung vom Sinaibund," *ZAW* 73 (1961) 137-146.

_____ *Einleitung in das Alten Testament*[3] (Tübingen: Mohr [Siebeck], 1964).

_____ *Hexateuch-synopse* (Leipzig: Hinrich, 1922).

_____ "Lade und Stierbild," *ZAW* 58 (1940-1) 190-215.

_____ *Das Lied Moses Deuteronomium 32 1-43 und das Lehrgedicht Asaphs Psalm 78 samt einer Analyse der Umgebung des Mose-Liedes* (Sachsische Akademie, philologisch-historische Klasse 104:5; Berlin: Akademie, 1958).

_____ "Zwei verkannte militär-technische Termini im Alten Testament," *VT* 5 (1955) 232-238.

Eliade, M., *The Myth of the Eternal Return* (Bollingen Series 46; New York: Random House, 1965).

Emerton, J. A., "'Spring and Torrent' in Psalm LXXIV 15," *Volume du congrès, Genève, 1965* (VTSup 15; Leiden: Brill, 1966) 122-133.

Ewald, H. A., *A Commentary on the Psalms* (2 vols.; Theological Translation Fund Library 24; London/Edinburh: Williams and Norgate, 1881).

Falkenstein, A., and von Soden, W., *Sumerische und akkadische Hymnen und Gebete* (Bibliothek der alten Welt; Zürich/Stuttgart: Artemis, 1953).

Fenton, T. L., "Ugaritica-Biblica," *UF* 1 (1969) 65-70.

Finkel, J., "Some Problems Relating to Ps. 95," *AJSLL* 50 (1933) 32-40.

Finkelstein, I.; Lederman, Ts.; Bonimonitch, Sh., "Shiloh, 1981," *IEJ* 32 (1982) 148-150.

_____ "Shiloh, 1983," *IEJ* 33 (1983) 267-268.

Fohrer, G., *Elia* (Abhandlungen zur Theologie des Alten und Neuen Testaments; Zürich: Zwingli, 1957).

Frankfort, H., *Cylinder Seals* (London: Macmillan, 1939).

Frazer, J. G., ed., *Apollodorus—The Library* (2 vols.; LCL; London: Heinemann, 1921).

_____ *Folklore in the Old Testament* (3 vols.; London: Macmillan, 1918).

Freedman, D. N., "Archaic Forms in Early Hebrew Poetry," *ZAW* 72 (1960) 101-107.

_____ "Divine Names and Titles in Early Hebrew Poetry," *Magnalia Dei* (Fs. G. E. Wright; eds. F. M. Cross, W. E. Lemke and P. D. Miller, Jr.; Garden City, New York: Doubleday, 1976) 55-107.

_____ "Psalm 113 and the Song of Hannah," *Pottery, Poetry, and Prophecy* (Winona Lake, Indiana: Eisenbrauns, 1980) 243-261.

_____ "The Structure of Isaiah 40:1-11" *Perspectives on Language and Text* (F.s. F. I. Andersen; ed. E. W. Conrad, E. G. Newing; Winona Lake, Indiana: Eisebrauns, forthcoming).

Friedman, R. E., *The Exile and Biblical Narrative* (HSM 22; Chico, California: Scholars Press, 1981).

Fritz, V., *Israel in der Wüste* (Marburger theologische Studien 7; Marburg: Elwert, 1970).

Gaster, T. H., *Thespis*[2] (New York: Schuman, 1950).

Ginsberg, H. L., *Kitbê 'Ûgārît* (Jerusalem: Bialik, 1936).

_____ "Two North-Canaanite Letters from Ugarit," *BASOR* 72 (1958) 18-19.

Gispen, W. H., *Exodus* (Bible Student's Commentary: Grand Rapids: Zondervan, 1982).

Gradwohl, P., "Die Verbrennung des Jungstiers, Ex. 32, 20," *TZ* 19 (1963) 50-53.

Gray, G. B., *A Critical and Exegetical Commentary on Numbers* (ICC; Edinburgh: Clark, 1903).

Gray, J., *I & II Kings* (OTL; Philadelphia, Pennsylvania: Westminster, 1963).

Greenberg, M., *Ezekiel 1-20* (AB 22; Garden City, New York: Doubleday, 1983).

_____ "*MSRT HBRYT*, 'The obligation of the covenant,' in Ezekiel 20:37," *The Word of the Lord Shall go Forth* (Fs. D. N. Freedman; Winona Lake, Indiana: Eisenbrauns, 1983) 37-46.

Greenfield, J. C., "Lexicographical Studies II," *HUCA* 30 (1959) 141-151.

Gressmann, H., *Mose und seine Zeit* (Göttingen: Vandenhoeck & Ruprecht, 1913).

Grønbaeck, J. H., "Juda und Amalek: Überlieferungsgeschichtliche Erwägungen zu Exodus 17, 18-16," *ST* 18 (1964) 26-45.

Grondahl, F., *Die Personennamen der Texte aus Ugarit* (Studia Pohl 1; Rome: PBI, 1967).

Gross, H., *Die Idee des ewigen und allgemeinen Weltfriedens im alten Orient und im Alten Testament* (Trierer theologische Studien 7; Trier: Paulinus, 1956).

Gunkel, H., *Genesis*[3] (Göttinger Handkommentar zum Alten Testament 1.1; Göttingen: Vandenhoeck & Ruprecht, 1910).

_____ *Die Psalmen* (Göttingen: Vandenhoeck & Ruprecht, 1929).

_____ *Schöpfung und Chaos in Urzeit und Endzeit* (Göttingen: Vandenhoeck & Ruprecht, 1895).

Gunneweg, A. H. J., *Leviten und Priester* (Göttingen: Vandenhoeck & Ruprecht, 1965).

Haldar, A., *The Notion of the Desert in Sumero-Akkadian and West-Semitic Religions* (Uppsala Universitets Årsskrift 1950:3; Uppsala: Almqvist & Wiksell, 1950).

Halpern, B., *The Constitution of the Monarchy in Israel* (HSM 25; Chico, California: Scholars Press, 1981).

_____ *The Emergence of Israel in Canaan* (SBL Monographs 29; Chico, California: Scholars Press, 1983).

Harner, P. B., "Creation Faith in Deutero-Isaiah," *VT* 17 (1967) 298-306.

Hempel, J., "'Ich bin der Herr, dein Arzt' (Ex 15,26)," *TLZ* 82 (1957) 809-826.

Hofbauer, J., "Psalm 77/78, ein 'politisch Lied'," *ZKT* 89 (1967) 41-50.

Hoffner, H. A., "The Elkunirsa Myth Reconsidered," *RHA* 23 (1965) 5-16.

Hölscher, G., "Zu Num 20:1-13," *ZAW* 45 (1927) 239-240.

Holzinger, H., *Einleitung in den Hexateuch* (Freiburg: Mohr [Siebeck], 1893).

_____ *Exodus* (Kurzer Hand-commentar zum Alten Testament 2; Tübingen: Mohr [Siebeck], 1900).

Huffmon, H. B., *Amorite Personal Names in the Mari Texts* (Baltimore: Hopkins, 1965).

Hurvitz, A., *Bên lāšôn lᵉlāšôn* (English title *The Transition Period in Biblical Hebrew*; Jerusalem: Bialik, 1972).

Hvidberg-Hansen, O., "Die Vernichtung des goldenes Kalbs und der ugaritischen Ernteritus," *ActOr* 33 (1971) 5-46.

Jackson, K. P., *The Ammonite Language of the Iron Age* (HSM 27; Chico, California; Scholars Press, 1983).

Janssen, E., *Juda in der Exilszeit* (Forschungen zur Religion und Literatur des Alten und Neuen Testaments; Göttingen: Vandenhoeck & Ruprecht, 1956).

Jenks, A., *The Elohist and North Israelite Tradition* (SBL Monographs 22; Missoula, Montana: Scholars Press, 1977).

Junker, H., "Die Entstehungszeit des Ps. 78 und des Deuteronomiums," *Bib* 34 (1953) 487-500.

Kapelrud, A. S., *Baal in the Ras Shamra Texts* (Copenhagen: Gad, 1952).

Kaufmann, Y., *The Babylonian Captivity and Deutero-Isaiah (History of the Religion of Israel* 4; Hebrew original 1937-1956; New York: Union of American Congregations, 1970).

Kiesow, K., *Exodustexte im Jesajabuch* (Orbis Biblicus et Orientalis 24; Göttingen: Vandenhoeck & Ruprecht, 1979).

Kirkpatrick, A. F., *The Book of Psalms* (3 vols.; Cambridge Bible for Schools and Colleges; Cambridge: University, 1901).

Kissane, E. J., *The Book of Psalms* (2 vols.; Westminster: Newman, 1953).

Kittel, R., *Die Psalmen* (KAT; Leipzig: Deichert, 1914).

Knight, D. A., *Rediscovering the Traditions of Israel* (SBL Dissertation 9; Missoula, Montana: Scholars Press, 1975).

Koenig, J., "Sourciers, thaumaturges et scribes," *RHR* 164 (1963) 17-38, 165-180.

Kohata, F., "Die priesterschriftliche Überlieferungsgeschichte von Numeri XX 1-13," *Annual of the Japanese Biblical Institute* 3 (1977) 3-34.

Kraus, H.-J., *Psalmen* (2 vols.; BKAT; Neukirchen: Neukirchener Verlag, 1960).

Labuschange, C. F., "The Tribes in the Blessing of Moses," *OTS* 19 (1974) 108-112.

Lagrange, M. J., *Le livre des juges* (Études Bibliques; Paris: Libraire Lecoffre, 1903).

Lambert, W. G., and Millard, A. R., *Atra-Ḫasis* (Oxford: Oxford, 1969).

Landsberger, B., "Jahreszeiten im Sumerisch-Akkadischen," *JNES* 8 (1949) 248-297.

Lehming, S., "Massa und Meriba," *ZAW* 73 (1961) 71-77.

_____"Versuch zu Ex. XXXII," *VT* 10 (1960) 16-50.

Levenson, J. D., *Theology of the Program of Restoration of Ezekiel 40-48* (HSM 10; Missoula, Montana: Scholars Press, 1976).

Loewenstamm, S. A., "*'Ēdût biyhôsēp,*" *Eretz-Israel* 5 (1958) 80-82.

_____"*Hannûshâ 'bā'ēt hahî'' bin'ûmê happ^{e}tiḥâ šel sēper d^{e}bārîm,*" *Tarbiz* 38 (1968-9) 99-104.

_____"*Haqd^{e}šat Lēwî la'ăbôdat h' b^{e}māsôrôt hattôrâ,*" *Eretz-Israel* 10 (1971) 169-172.

_____"The Making and Destruction of the Golden Calf," *Bib* 48 (1967) 481-490.

_____"The Making and Destruction of the Golden Calf—a Rejoinder," *Bib* 56 (1975) 330-343.

_____"*Maṭṭe(h),*" *'Enṣiqlôpedyâ Miqrā'ît* 4, 825-832.

_____"Ugaritic Formulas of Greeting," *BASOR* 194 (1969) 52-54.

Lohfink, N., "'Ich bin Jahwe, dein Arzt' (Ex 15,26)," "*Ich will euer Gott werden*" (SBS 100; Stuttgart: Katholisches Bibelwerk, 1981) 13-73.

Long, B. O., *The Problem of Etiological Narrative in the Old Testament* (BZAW 108; Berlin: Töpelmann, 1968).

Lord, A. B., *The Singer of Tales* (Harvard Studies in Comparative Literature 24; Cambridge, Massachusetts: Harvard, 1960).

Loza, J., "Exode XXXII et la redaction JE," *VT* 23 (1973) 31-55.

Luria, B.-Z., "*Mizmôrê t^{e}hillîm mē'eprayim,*" *Beth Mikra* 23 (1978) 151-161.

McNeile, A. H., *The Book of Exodus*^{2} (Westminster Commentaries; London: Methuen, 1917). (1971) 374-400.

Margaliot, M. "*Ḥēṭ(') Mōše(h) w^e'ahărôn b^{e}mê M^{e}rîbâ,*" *Beth Mikra* 19 (1971) 374-400.

May, H. G., "Some Cosmic Connotations of *Mayim Rabbîm,* 'Many Waters'," *JBL* 74 (1955) 9-21.

Mendenhall, G. E., "Samuel's 'Broken *Rib*': Deuteronomy 32," *No Famine in the Land* (Fs. J. L. McKenzie; eds. J. W. Flanagan and A. W. Robinson; Missoula, Montana: Scholars Press, 1975).

Mercati, G., *Psalterii Hexapli Reliquiae* (Codices ex Ecclesiasticis Italiae Bibliothecis 8; Rome: Vatican Library, 1958).

Meyer, E., *Die Israeliten und ihre Nachbarstämme* (The Halle: Niemeyer, 1906).

Meyer, R., "Die Bedeutung von Deuteronomium 32,8f.43 (4Q) für die Auslegung des Moseliedes," *Verbannung und Heimkehr* (Fs. W. Rudolph; ed. A. Kuschke; Tübingen: Mohr [Siebeck], 1961) 197-209.

Miller, P. D., "'El, The Creator of Earth," *BASOR* 239 (1980) 43-46.

Miqrā'ôt G^{e}dôlôt (Jerusalem: Pardes, 1954).

Montgomery, J. A., *The Books of Kings* (ICC; Edinburgh: Clark, 1951).

Moor, J. C. de, *The Seasonal Pattern in the Ugaritic Myth of Ba'lu* (AOAT 16; Neukirchenk-Vluyn: Kevelaer, 1971).

Moran, W. L., "A Kingdom of Priests," *The Bible in Modern Catholic Thought* (ed. J. L. McKenzie; New York: Herder and Herder, 1962) 7-20.

_____ "Some Remarks on the Song of Moses," *Bib* 43 (1962) 317-327.

Myers, J. M., *Ezra-Nehemiah* (AB 14; Garden City, New York: Doubleday, 1965).

Negoiță, A., Ringgren, H., "*Dāšan,*" *TWAT* 2, 331-334.

Nelson, R. D., *The Double Redaction of the Deuteronomistic History* (Sheffield: JSOT, 1981).

Nicholson, E. W., *The Book of the Prophet Jeremiah Chapters 26-52* (Cambridge Bible Commentary; Cambridge: University, 1975).

Noth, M., *Geschichte Israels*^{5} (Göttingen: Vandenhoeck & Ruprecht, 1963).

_____ *Überlieferungsgeschichte des Pentateuch* (Stuttgart: Kohlhammer, 1948).

_____ *Überlieferungsgeschichtliche Studien* 1 (Schriften der königsberger gelehrten Gesellschaft, Geisteswissenschaftliche Klasse 18:2; The Halle: Niemeyer, 1943).

_____ *Das vierte Buch Mose. Numeri* (ATD 7; Göttingen: Vandenhoeck & Ruprecht, 1966).

_____ *Das zweite Buch Mose. Exodus* (ATD 5; Göttingen: Vandenhoeck & Ruprecht, 1968).

Oesterly, W. O. E., *The Psalms* (2 vols.; London: Society for Promoting Christian Knowledge, 1939).

Otten, H., "Ein kanaanäischer Mythus aus Boğasköy," *Mitteilungen des Instituts für Orientforschung* 1 (1953) 125-150.

Parrot, A., "Les peintures du palais de Mari," *Syria* 18 (1937) 325-354.

Patai, R., "The 'Control of Rain' in Ancient Palestine," *HUCA* 14 (1939) 251-286.

Patch, H. R., *The Other World According to Descriptions in Medieval Literature* (Smith College Studies in Modern Languages, N.S. 1; Cambridge, Massachusetts: Harvard, 1950).

Paul, S., "Literary and Ideological Echoes of Jeremiah in Deutero-Isaiah," *World Congress of Jewish Studies, Fifth*, 1 (4 vols.; Jerusalem: World Union of Jewish Studies, 1969) 102-120.

Pedersen, J., *Israel: Its Life and Culture* (2 vols.; Danish original 1920; London: Oxford, 1926).

Perlitt, L., "Sinai und Horeb," *Beiträge zur Altestamentlichen Theologie* (Fs. W. Zimmerli: eds. H. Donner, R. Hanhart and R. Smend; Göttingen: Vandenhoeck & Ruprecht, 1977) 302-322.

Perdue, L. G., "The Making and Destruction of the Golden Calf—A Reply," *Bib* 54 (1973) 237-246.

Pope, M., *El in the Ugaritic Texts* (VTSup 2; Leiden: Brill, 1955).

_____ "Isaiah 34 in Relation to Isaiah 35, 40-66," *JBL* 71 (1952) 235-243.

_____ *Job*^{3} (AB 15; Garden City, New York: Doubleday, 1973).

Propp, William H., "On Hebrew *Śāde(h)*, 'Highland'," *VT* (forthcoming).

_____ "The Rod of Aaron and the Sin of Moses," *JBL* (forthcoming).

Qimron, E., *"Hahabhānâ bên wāw l^{e}yôd bit'ûdôt midbar Y^{e}hûdâ,"* *Beth Mikra* 18 (1972) 102-112.

von Rad, G., *Gesammelte Studien zum Alten Testament* (Theologische Bücherei 8; Munich: Kaiser, 1958).

Rendtorff, R., "Die theologische Stellung des Schöpfungsglaubens bei Deuterojesaja," *ZTK* 51 (1954) 3-13.

Reymond, P., *L'eau, sa vie, et sa signification dans l'Ancien Testament* (VTSup 6; Leiden: Brill, 1958).

Riemann, P. A., "Desert and Return to Desert in the Pre-exilic Prophets" (Harvard diss., 1964).

Robertson, D. A., *Linguistic Evidence in Dating Early Hebrew Poetry* (SBL Dissertation 3; Missoula, Montana: Scholars, 1972).

Rössler, O., "Ghain im Ugaritischen," *ZA* 54 (1961) 158-172.

Rudolph, W., *Der "Elohist" von Exodus bis Josua* (Berlin: Töpelmann, 1938).

_____ *Esra und Nehemiah* (HAT 20; Tübingen: Mohr [Siebeck], 1949).

Rundgren, F., "Zum Lexicon des Alten Testaments," *ActOr* 21 (1953) 301-345.

Saebø, M., "Die hebräischen Nomina 'ed und 'ēd," *ST* 24 (1970) 130-141.

Sachsse, E., "Der jahwistische Schöpfungsbericht," *ZAW* 39 (1921) 281-282.

Schmidt, W. H., *Exodus, Sinai und Mose* (Erträge der Forschung 191; Darmstadt: Wissenschaftliche Buchgesellschaft, 1983).

Seebass H., *Mose und Aaron, Sinai und Gottesberg* (Abhandlungen zur evanglelischen Theologie 2; Bonn: Bouvier, 1962).

Sellin, E., "Wann wurde das Moselied Dtn 32 gedichtet?" *ZAW* 43 (1925) 161-173.

Skehan, P. W., "Qumran and the Present State of Old Testament Studies: the Masoretic Text," *JBL* 78 (1959) 21-33.

Skinner, J., *Genesis*[2] (ICC; Edinburgh: Clark, 1930).

Smith, M., "*Běrît 'Am/Běrît 'Ôlām*: A New Proposal for the Crux of Isaiah 42:6," *JBL* 100 (1981) 241-243.

Smith, W. Robertson, *Lectures on the Religion of the Semites*[2] (London: Black, 1914).

Snaith, N. H., *Leviticus and Numbers* (Century Bible; London: Nelson, 1967).

Soden, W. von, "Kleine Beiträge zum Ugaritischen und Hebräischen," *Hebräische Wortforschung* (Fs. W. Baumgartner; VTSup 16; Leiden: Brill, 1967) 291-300.

Speiser, E. A., "*'Ed* in the Story of Creation," *BASOR* 140 (1955) 9-11.

_____ *Genesis* (AB 1; Garden City, New York: Doubleday, 1964).

Stuhlmueller, C., *Psalms* (2 vols.; Old Testament Message 22; Wilmington, Delaware: Glazier, 1983).

_____ "The Theology of Creation in Second Isaias," *CBQ* 21 (1959) 429-467.

Thompson, S., *Motif-index of Folk-literature* (6 vols.; Bloomington, Indiana: Indiana University, 1955).

Tigay, J. H., *The Evolution of the Gilgamesh Epic* (Philadelphia, Pennsylvania: University of Pennsylvania, 1982).

_____ "'Heavy of Mouth' and 'Heavy of Tongue': On Moses' Speech Difficulty," *BASOR* 231 (1978) 57-67.

Tournay, R., "Les psaumes complexes (suite)," *RB* 56 (1949) 37-60.

Trever, J. C., "Isaiah 43:19 According to the First Isaiah Scroll (DSIa)," *BASOR* 121 (1951) 13-16.

Tromp, N. J., *Primitive Conceptions of Death and the Nether World in the Old Testament* (Biblica et Orientalia 21; Rome: PBI, 1969).

Tsevat, M., "The Canaanite God Šälaḥ," *VT* 4 (1954) 41-49.

van Uchelen, N. A., "Abraham als Felsen (Jes 51 1)," *ZAW* 80 (1968) 183-190.

van Zijl, P. J., *Baal* (AOAT 10; Neukirchen-Vluyn: Neukirchener Verlag, 1972).

de Vaulx, J., *Les Nombres* (Sources Bibliques; Paris: Gabalda, 1972).

de Vaux, R., *Histoire ancienne d'Israël* (2 vols.; Paris: Lecoffre, 1971-3).

Watson, P. L., "Mot, the God of Death, at Ugarit and in the Old Testament," (Yale diss., 1970).

Weimar, P., *Die Berufung des Mose* (Orbis Biblicus et Orientalis 32; Göttingen: Vandenhoeck & Ruprecht, 1980).

Weinberg, S., "*'Ereṣ-Yiśrā'ēl 'aḥărê ḥorban bayit ri(')šôn*," *Proceedings of the Israel Academy of Science and Humanities* 4 (Jerusalem: Israel Academy of Science and Humanites, 1971) 202-216.

Weiser, A., *Die Psalmen* (ATD 14/15; Göttingen: Vandenhoeck & Ruprecht, 1966).

Wellhausen, J., *Prolegomena zur Geschichte Israels*[6] (Berlin: Reimer, 1905).

_____ *Skizzen und Vorarbeiten* (6 vols.; Berlin: Reimer, 1884-1899).

Wernberg-Møller, P., "Two Difficult Passages in the Old Testament," *ZAW* 69 (1957) 69-73.

Westermann, C., *Isaiah 40-66* (German original 1966; OTL; Philadelphia, Pennsylvania: Westminster, 1969).

Wiseman, D. J., *The Vassal-Treaties of Esarhaddon* (London: Harrison, 1958).

_____ *Joel and Amos* (German original 1969; Hermeneia; Philadelphia, Pennsylvania: Fortress, 1977).

Wright, G. E., "Deuteronomy, Introduction," *IB* 2, 311-330.

_____ "The Lawsuit of God: A Form-Critical Study of Deuteronomy 32," *Israel's Prophetic Heritage* (Fs. J. Muilenberg; eds. B. W. Anderson and W. Harrelson; New York: Harper, 1962) 26-67.

Zenger, E., *Israel am Sinai* (Altenberge: CIS, 1982).

Ziegler, J., *Isaias*[3] (Göttingen Septuagint 14; Göttingen: Vandenhoeck & Ruprecht, 1983).

Zimmerli, W., *Ezekiel* (2 vols.; BKAT 13; Neukirchen: Neukirchener Verlag, 1969).

_____ "Ich bin Jahwe," *Geschichte und Altes Testament* (Fs. A. Alt; Beiträge zur historischen Theologie 16; Tübingen: Mohr [Siebeck], 1953).

_____ "Der 'neue Exodus' in der Verkundigung der beiden grossen Exilspropheten" (1960), *Gottes Offenbarung* (Theologische Bücherei 19; Munich: Kaiser, 1963) 192-204.

Zobel, H. J., *Stammespruch und Geschichte* (BZAW 95; Berlin: Töpelmann, 1965).